A Basic Guide to
EVIDENCE
IN
CRIMINAL CASES

The Honourable
Roger E. Salhany

CARSWELL
Toronto • Calgary • Vancouver
1990

Canadian Cataloguing in Publication Data

Salhany, Roger E.
  A basic guide to evidence in criminal cases

Includes bibliographical references.
ISBN 0-459-34781-0

1. Evidence, Criminal — Canada.   I. Title.

KE9312.S35 1990   345.71'06   C90-095106-0

Typesetting: Video Text Inc., Barrie, Ontario, Canada

To Terri

Preface

Trying to learn the law of evidence is like trying to learn a new language. For every rule there is usually an exception, and for each exception there is often an additional exception. This is probably because what the rules of evidence seek to achieve is a delicate balance between probity and fairness. However, when we look more closely, we discover that too often the rules or exceptions are based on historical anachronisms or public policy rather than common sense.

This book purports to be nothing more than its title suggests. It is a guide, not a text book. Its purpose is to explain not only what kinds of evidence are permitted in a criminal trial but, more importantly, why certain rules exclude evidence that common sense tells us might assist in the discovery of the truth. It is offered to police officers, social workers, investigators, law students and anyone interested in understanding what goes on in the court room.

I want to express my gratitude to my venerable colleague, Judge Costello who kindly shared his experience of thirty years as a trial judge, and to Professor Syd Usprich for his many scholarly suggestions and grammatical corrections. Once more, I want to thank Irene Parker who found time in her very busy schedule to type the manuscript.

New Dundee, July 23, 1990   R.E.S.

Table of Contents

Table of Cases

PART I

Admissibility

1

General Principles

1. INTRODUCTION

In every criminal case, there are three things that the Crown must establish in order to succeed in proving its case. The first is that a crime was committed (what lawyers call the *actus reus*). The second is that the accused standing in the prisoner's dock committed the crime (what is known as identity). The third and final thing that must be established is that the accused intended to commit the crime, in the sense that it was his deliberate act. This is what is called *mens rea*. It is not to be confused with motive because why a person commits a crime is not really something with which a court concerns itself, although it may be relevant as evidence to prove identity. There are also certain crimes where intention is not relevant; sometimes the person may not even be aware that he was committing the crime. These are called strict liability offences and are not necessary to this discussion.

Therefore, the first question that a lawyer involved in a case, whether the prosecutor or the defence counsel, must ask is this: what does a particular piece of evidence prove? This is the very question that a police officer must ask when called upon to investigate a crime after arrival at the scene. As the officer looks over the crime scene, he or she will make a number of observations. There may be items such as weapons, broken windows, footprints or injured parties which will arouse suspicion. Persons may come forward and give a statement about their observations. The officer will be advised of certain information and will conduct an investigation that may turn up objects or statements which may or may not be relevant to the case. The officer must continually keep in mind the question, "What does all of this prove?"

2. TEST OF RELEVANCY

As I said earlier, there are three issues which the Crown must prove in every criminal case: the act, the identity, and the intent. With these three issues of proof (and these issues alone), we can formulate a rule or test of admissibility. The rule is simply this: evidence is admissible if it is relevant to one of the three issues mentioned above. If it is, then it is said to be logically probative so long as it is not contrary to one of the rules that may exclude evidence, and which will be discussed later. Sometimes, however, not every piece of evidence which is of probative value, even if it is not contrary to an exlusionary rule, will be automatically admitted. If its probative value is slight, and that value is outweighed by its prejudice or confusion of the jury, then the trial judge may exclude it. He or she does so in order to ensure that the accused will have a fair trial.

Let me give you an example. Let us assume that a man is charged with the sexual assault of a young girl and there is evidence that he committed a similar crime five years earlier using the same method. The Crown may argue that the evidence of the previous offence is relevant to one of the three issues. What the trial judge must decide, first of all, is whether it is relevant and probative of the issues in the case before him. It may or may not be. Assuming that it is, a trial judge must next consider whether its prejudice outweighs its probative value. Why is it prejudicial? It is prejudicial because the jury (and even the judge) may be swayed more by the fact that he committed a crime on a previous occasion than the issue before them, namely, whether he committed the particular crime which he is now facing.

A well-known case where the question of prejudice arose is the English "Brides in the Bath" case.[1] There, the accused (Smith) was charged with the murder of his wife, who was found dead in their bathtub filled with water, under circumstances that were consistent with accident. He was the beneficiary of her small estate. There was further evidence that Smith had married two other women who had died under identical circumstances and by whose death he had profited. It is highly unlikely that three wives would die accidentally in a bathtub. On the other hand, it is obvious that such evidence was highly prejudicial. Here, the trial judge concluded that the probative value of such evidence far outweighed its prejudicial value

---

1   *R. v. Smith* (1915), 11 Cr. App. R. 229 (C.C.A.).

and admitted the circumstances of the two previous deaths. Not surprisingly, Smith was convicted and sentenced to hang, and his conviction was upheld by the English Court of Criminal Appeal.

3. EVIDENCE WHICH MAY BE EXCLUDED

The general rule at common law was that apart from the question of confessions, the court was not concerned with how evidence was obtained. So long as the evidence was relevant to a fact in issue, the court allowed the evidence to be admitted.

In the last fifty years, however, Canadian and English courts have become concerned about whether courts have and should have a discretion to exclude evidence which is otherwise admissible, where it would operate unfairly to the accused. In *R. v. Wray*,[2] the Supreme Court of Canada indicated that it was prepared to recognize a limited discretion but only where the evidence had very little probative value and was also gravely prejudicial to the accused.

The Canadian Charter of Rights and Freedoms[3] enacted in 1982 has substantially broadened the power of the courts to exclude evidence where a right or freedom guaranteed by the Charter has been denied or infringed. Section 24 provides:

> 24(1) Anyone whose rights or freedoms, as guaranteed by this Charter, have been infringed or denied may apply to a court of competent jurisdiction to obtain such remedy as the court considers appropriate and just in the circumstances.

> (2) Where, in proceedings under subsection (1), a court concludes that evidence was obtained in a manner that infringed or denied any rights or freedoms guaranteed by this Charter, *the evidence shall be excluded* if it is established that, having regard to all the circumstances, the admission of it in the proceedings would bring the administration of justice into disrepute. (Emphasis added).

---

2 [1970] 4 C.C.C. 1, 11 C.R.N.S. 235 (S.C.C.).

3 Part I of the Constitution Act, 1982, being Schedule B of the Canada Act, 1982 (U.K.), 1982, c. 11.

2

Kinds of Evidence

1. INTRODUCTION

The law recognizes two methods of proof: direct evidence and circumstantial evidence. There is no particular magic in these terms. Direct evidence is simply evidence which directly proves a fact in issue. For example, if the fact in issue is whether Smith stabbed Jones, a witness who testifies that he saw Smith stab Jones is giving what is known as direct evidence.

Circumstantial evidence, on the other hand, is evidence of surrounding circumstances from which an inference may be drawn that a certain fact occurred. Let us take our previous example of Smith and Jones and let us assume that the witness did not see Smith stab Jones. Instead, he observed Smith walking down the street with a knife in his hand all covered in blood and saw Jones, a short distance away, lying in a pool of blood. The witness did not see Smith stab Jones but it is a reasonable inference from all of the surrounding circumstances that Smith did in fact do so. This is what is described as circumstantial evidence, as opposed to direct evidence, of a fact in issue.

Though both types of evidence are permitted, a court scrutinizes circumstantial evidence more carefully. The burden of proof will be discussed in a subsequent chapter. It is only necessary at this stage to say that the burden of proof is on the Crown to prove the guilt of an accused and such proof must be established beyond a reasonable doubt. When proof is based on circumstantial evidence either in whole or in part, a judge will usually caution a jury (or himself where he is trying the case alone) that before they can rely on circumstantial evidence, they must be satisfied that the guilt of the accused is the only logical inference to be drawn from such evidence.

There are three types of evidence that are generally recognized as admissible to establish a fact in issue. They are: oral testimony or *viva voce* evidence; real evidence which includes documents or things such as weapons, etc.; and demonstrative evidence which includes photographs, maps, etc.

2. ORAL TESTIMONY

(a) Generally

The most common way that evidence is given is by a witness entering the witness box and testifying in open court. In Canada, as well as throughout other common law jurisdictions, the order of questioning a witness is strictly controlled. The witness is first examined by the side who calls him; he may then be cross-examined by the other side; and finally he may be re-examined by the first side. Unlike the continental system, which allows a witness to repeat his evidence with little interruption, the evidence of a witness is tightly controlled by the questions asked. This does not mean that the witness must either answer yes or no. However, the practice is for the witness to be asked a question and for him to be required to respond to it. In short, he must respond to the question and not make a speech unconnected with that question.

There is a distinction, however, in the type of questions that may be asked in chief (that is by the person who calls the witness), and the questions that might be asked in cross-examination (that is by the person who is on the other side). When a witness is examined in chief, the examiner must not lead him nor suggest the answer to him. On the other hand, cross-examination may suggest answers to the witness. The purpose of cross-examination is to test the accuracy of what the witness has said in chief. It is also to bring out new evidence that the witness did not give in chief. Once cross-examination is completed, the side that called the witness is entitled to re-examine him. Re-examination is restricted solely to matters that were raised in cross-examination and is allowed in order to clarify those answers that were given.

(b) Competency

Not everyone is allowed to enter the witness box and to give oral evidence. A person called as a witness must be competent to give testimony. Until the end of the last century, there were a great many individuals who were considered not competent to give evidence. For example, a person might not be allowed to testify because he had an interest in the case and therefore his evidence was not considered reliable. In fact, it was not until 1640 that a person charged with a felony, (i.e., a serious crime), was allowed to call witnesses for the defence. And until the end of that century, witnesses for the defence were not allowed to give their evidence under oath. The theory was that such witnesses, if they contradicted the witnesses for the prosecution, were probably lying. The most serious restriction was that the accused himself was not allowed to testify, again for the same reason. It was not until 1898, less than a hundred years ago, that an accused in England was allowed to give evidence under oath on his own behalf. In Canada, that right was granted a few years earlier. Section 3 of the Canada Evidence Act[1] specifically provides that "a person is not incompetent to give evidence by reason of interest or crime."

Another person who was not allowed to give evidence was the spouse of an accused. This was based on the theory that husband and wife were one and, if the accused was incompetent to testify, so was his spouse. Another reason for the rule was the natural repugnance of using the law to compel a wife to betray her husband or *vice versa*. The rule applied even if the parties were not husband and wife at the time of the offence,

---

1 R.S.C. 1985, c. C-5.

so long as they were married at the time of the trial.[2] Ironically, the same rule was not applied to prevent children from betraying a parent, or a sister or brother from betraying a sibling.

The rule which rendered a spouse incompetent was abolished in Canada at the end of the last century by section 4 of the Canada Evidence Act. The law today is that a spouse is competent to testify on behalf of the defence, but not for the prosecution except in those instances specified in subsections 2 and 4 of section 4, or where the offence charged affects his or her health or liberty.

Today, generally all witnesses are competent to testify if they understand the nature and consequences of an oath. When a person takes an oath it means that he understands the moral obligation to tell the truth.[3] For a long period of time, those who would not or could not take an oath because of their religion, or lack of it, were not allowed to testify.

In Canada, an oath is no longer required. Section 14 of the Canada Evidence Act allows someone to affirm if the traditional oath is objected to on the grounds of conscientious scruples or because the person would not be bound by it. In such an instance, the person is required to solemnly affirm that the evidence to be given by him "shall be the truth, the whole truth and nothing but the truth." This means that if the witness tells a lie, he is liable to prosecution for perjury just as if he had taken the traditional oath.

(c) Witnesses Who May Not Be Competent

Section 16 of the Canada Evidence Act contemplates that there are two persons who may not be competent to give evidence: the first is a person under the age of 14 years; and the second is a person who is mentally incompetent. Whenever the testimony of such a person is challenged, the court is required, before permitting the person to give evidence, to conduct an inquiry to determine: (1) whether the person understands the nature of an oath or solemn affirmation; and (2) whether the person is able to communicate the evidence. If the court is satisfied that both conditions are met, then the witness will be entitled to give evidence under oath or solemn affirmation (section 16(2)).

However, the fact that the proposed witness does not understand the nature of an oath or a solemn affirmation will not necessarily exclude his testimony. Provided that the witness is "able to communicate the

---

2 *Hoskyn v. Metropolitan Police Commissioner* (1978), 67 Cr. App. R. 88 (H.L.).

3 *R. v. Fletcher* (1982), 1 C.C.C. (3d) 370 (Ont. C.A.), leave to appeal to S.C.C. refused (1983), 48 N.R. 319 (S.C.C.).

evidence" and promises to tell the truth, he will be allowed to testify (section 16(3)).[4]

The test, therefore, is the ability to communicate the evidence. Such evidence, particularly in the case of a very young child or a lunatic, may be unreliable. However, that does not necessarily mean that the evidence must not be received. The question of its reliability will be go to the weight that must be given to such testimony and in some instances, very little weight may be given to it.

(d) Compellability

To say that a witness is compellable means that he may be called by either side to give evidence. However, the fact that a person may be competent to testify does not necessarily mean that he is compellable to testify. Although the general rule is that all competent witnesses are also compellable, there are a number of exceptions.

The most notable exception is the accused. Although an accused is competent to testify, he is not compellable. However, if he elects to testify, he cannot refuse to answer questions which may incriminate him. He must submit to cross-examination on any issue relating to the case, subject to a limited discretion in the trial judge to prevent cross-examination on a previous criminal record.[5]

A person jointly charged and tried with other accused is not compellable either by the prosecution or by a co-accused. However, if a person jointly charged is tried separately, he becomes an ordinary witness and may be compelled to testify by the prosecution or by the accused who is on trial.

When an accused's spouse was made a competent witness for the defence, he or she was also made a compellable witness for the defence. However, since a spouse is not competent to testify for the prosecution, he or she is also not compellable to testify for the prosecution. There are two exceptions to the rule. The first is the common law exception, preserved by section 4(5) of the Canada Evidence Act, that the prosecution can call the accused's spouse as a witness without the accused's consent where the common law permitted it. The common law made it an exception where the evidence disclosed that the spouse's person, liberty or health had been threatened by the accused spouse. Sections 4(2) and 4(4) make husbands and wives compellable against one another with respect to certain offences specified in those sections. The purpose is to ensure that spouses will testify against one another where an offence has been committed

---

4 *R. v. D. (R.R.)* (1989), 47 C.C.C. (3d) 97, 69 C.R. (3d) 267 (Sask. C.A.).

5 *R. v. Corbett* (1988), 41 C.C.C. (3d) 385, 64 C.R. (3d) 1 (S.C.C.).

against children, particularly their own. Before the enactment of these sections, children who had been physically or sexually assaulted could not count upon one parent to testify against the other parent who had been charged with committing the offence.

(e) Refreshing the Witness's Memory

A witness, who is called weeks, months, or even years after an event, may find that once he steps into the witness box, his memory has failed him on some critical issues. The rule is that a witness may refresh his memory while in the witness box from any record of the event which he has with him, provided:

(1) that he made the note of the event himself or, if it was made by another person, he verified the accuracy of the other person's note; and

(2) the note was written by him, or the record of another person was verified shortly after the event.

The reason for this rule is obvious. If a person has no memory of an event or just a faint one and must use notes to refresh it, then he is not recounting to the court what he clearly recalls but is essentially reading to the court what he once recorded. It is therefore important that what he recorded is accurate. The best way to ensure that it is accurate is for the person to have recorded it himself or to have verified the accuracy of someone else's record shortly after the event occurred. Ironically, the law does not permit the record to be admitted as evidence even though what the witness may be doing is simply reciting what is in his notes. In the past, some judges have even suggested that a witness should not rely on his notes while testifying in open court, which only encourages that witness to memorize those notes before he is called to testify.

Is the witness required to produce those notes for cross-examination? At one time, the rule was that a witness was only required to produce his notes if he relied upon them while testifying in court; if he used them to refresh his memory before court, they were not admissible. The irrationality of this distinction is self-evident. All it did was to encourage witnesses to memorize their notes before they came to court.

Today, it is generally accepted that any witness who refreshes his memory from notes prior to trial, or uses them to assist him during his testimony, must produce them to the opposing counsel for cross-examination.[6] This approach makes more sense. If a witness refreshes his memory before trial or relies upon the notes at trial, then what he says when he gives testimony is essentially the information in those notes.

---

6 *R. v. Catling* (1984), 29 C.C.C. (3d) 168 (Alta. C.A.).

Opposing counsel should be allowed to examine the notes to consider whether they are consistent with the witness's oral testimony. He may also wish to attack the accuracy of the notes by questioning the timeliness of the record and the possibility of invention.

(f) Adverse or Hostile Witnesses

As was pointed out earlier, the side who calls a witness is not allowed to ask that witness leading questions, that is, questions that directly or indirectly suggest the answer to the witness. Occasionally, however, counsel may discover that his witness has had a lapse of memory or that his testimony is inconsistent with a previous oral or written statement. This situation may be remedied by simply showing the witness his previous written statement and asking him to read it over. When this happens, he is in effect being allowed to refresh his memory. If he still insists that he cannot recall the information in the statement or says that it is incorrect, or even goes so far as to suggest that it was obtained as a result of a threat or inducement, then counsel is entitled to bring an application under section 9 of the Canada Evidence Act. That section provides:

> 9 (1) A party producing a witness shall not be allowed to impeach his credit by general evidence of bad character, but if the witness, in the opinion of the court, proves adverse, the party may contradict him by other evidence, or, by leave of the court, may prove that the witness made at other times a statement inconsistent with his present testimony, but before the last mentioned proof can be given the circumstances of the supposed statement, sufficient to designate the particular occasion, shall be mentioned to the witness, and he shall be asked whether or not he did make the statement.
>
> (2) Where the party producing a witness alleges that the witness made at other times a statement in writing, or reduced to writing, inconsistent with his present testimony, the court may, without proof that the witness is adverse, grant leave to that party to cross-examine the witness as to the statement and the court may consider the cross-examination in determining whether in the opinion of the court the witness is adverse.

It is obvious that this section has been badly drafted. It appears to require the court to make a finding that the witness is "adverse" before evidence may be called to demonstrate that he made a previous inconsistent statement (which will assist the court in reaching a decision on whether the witness is "adverse"). Fortunately, the courts have ignored the bad draftsmanship and have adopted a procedure that accords with logic and common sense.

In *R. v. Milgaard*,[7] the Saskatchewan Court of Appeal proposed the following procedure to be followed where this situation arises:

---

7 (1971), 2 C.C.C. (2d) 206, 14 C.R.N.S. 34, leave to appeal to S.C.C. refused (1971), 4 C.C.C. (2d) 566n (S.C.C.).

(1) Counsel should advise the court that he desires to make an application under s. 9 (2) of the *Canada Evidence Act.*

(2) When the court is so advised, the court should direct the jury to retire.

(3) Upon retirement of the jury, counsel should advise the trial judge of the particulars of the application and produce for him the alleged statement in writing or the writing to which the statement has been reduced.

(4) The learned trial judge should read the statement, or writing, and determine whether, in fact, there is an inconsistency between such statement or writing and the evidence the witness has given in court. If the learned trial judge decides there is no inconsistency, then that is the end of the matter. If he finds there is an inconsistency, he should then call upon counsel to prove the statement or writing.

(5) Counsel should then prove the statement or writing. This may be done by producing the statement or writing to the witness. If the witness admits the statement, or the statement reduced to writing, such proof would be sufficient. If the witness does not so admit, counsel should then provide the necessary proof by other evidence.

(6) If the witness admits making the statement, counsel for the opposing party should have the right to cross-examine as to the circumstances under which the statement was made. A similar right to cross-examine should be granted if the statement is proved by other witnesses. It may be that he will be able to establish that there were circumstances which would render it improper for the learned trial judge to permit the cross-examination, notwithstanding the apparent inconsistencies. The opposing counsel, too, should have the right to call evidence as to factors relevant to obtaining the statement, for the purpose of attempting to show that cross-examination should not be permitted.

(7) The learned trial judge should then decide whether or not he will permit the cross-examination. If so, the jury should be recalled.[8]

Two matters should be stressed at this point. Until the witness is declared adverse, cross-examination is limited to the statement that counsel says is a previous inconsistent statement. However, once the court rules that the witness is adverse, he may then be cross-examined at large, that is, on his entire evidence.

Finally, it is important to note that in deciding whether a person is adverse, the court is not restricted to relying only on the inconsistency in his testimony or the answers that he gives. The court may determine that a witness is adverse or, what is commonly called "hostile," by observing his general attitude or demeanour in the witness stand and the substance of his evidence.

If a witness has been found by the court to be adverse or "hostile"

---

8 *Ibid.,* at 221.

(or even if the court only permits him to be cross-examined because his testimony is inconsistent with his previous statement), the previous statement may be used in one of two ways. If during cross-examination the witness admits the truth of his earlier statement, then the trier of fact is entitled to accept the version of the evidence as contained in the prior statement. However, if the witness maintains the truth of his present evidence and insists that his earlier statement is incorrect, the trier is not entitled to accept the earlier statement as containing the truthful version of the events.

What is contained in a written statement is not evidence unless adopted by the witness even though, ironically, it was made at a time closer to the event and when the event was fresh in the witness's mind. As was pointed out earlier, our law only accepts testimony given out of the mouth of the witness even though that testimony is given weeks, months, or even years after the event. The only use that can be made of the previous statement is for the trier to reject the witness's present oral testimony because it is inconsistent with his previous statement; in other words, the earlier statement may be considered as having cancelled out his present oral testimony.

(g) Protection or Privilege from Answering Questions

When a witness enters the witness box, he is required to answer all questions that are relevant to the facts in issue. The common law, however, has recognized that for reasons of public policy, certain persons should be protected from answering questions touching on certain matters. It does not mean that the questions asked by examining counsel nor the answers he seeks are not relevant to the issues in the case. They may be very relevant. It simply means that the courts have concluded that society, as a whole, would be better served if certain witnesses were protected from revealing certain information even though that information was important and crucial to the determination of the case.

What kind of information is protected?

(i) *The Privilege Against Self-Incrimination*

Historically, anyone accused of hearsay or some other crime could be brought before a judge or some other public official and ordered to take an oath to answer truthfully all questions that might be put to him. He was not told of the specific crime that he was suspected to have committed nor the names of the witnesses against him. If he refused to take the oath or answer the questions put to him, he was thrown into prison and kept there until he agreed to answer the questions.

By the beginning of the seventeenth century, many persons summoned for questioning refused to take the oath and claimed that "no man should be required to incriminate himself." The prosecution of John Lilburne brought the matter to the attention of the courts and Parliament and, by the end of the seventeenth century, the claim of privilege became firmly established in all courts. It was enshrined in the American Bill of Rights as the Fifth Amendment on September 25th, 1789. In Canada, it was given constitutional recognition by section 11(c) of the Canadian Charter of Rights and Freedoms[9] in 1982. Section 11(c) provides:

11. Any person charged with an offence has the right

(c) not to be compelled to be a witness in proceedings against that person in respect of the offence.

Section 11(c) thus protects an accused from being forced to enter the witness box to give evidence. However, if he voluntarily chooses to testify, he loses his privilege of silence. He is required to answer all questions that are put to him by counsel or the judge, and any testimony that he gives may be considered by the judge and jury in determining his guilt or innocence on the charge. However, his testimony at that trial cannot be used against him in any other prosecution or proceeding against him except in a later prosecution for giving false testimony or contradictory evidence. This protection is similar to those already enjoyed under the Canada Evidence Act and under provincial evidence statutes. It was given constitutional recognition by section 13 of the Charter.

Section 13 provides:

A witness who testifies in any proceedings has the right not to have any incriminating evidence so given used to incriminate the witness in any other proceedings, except in a prosecution for perjury or for the giving of contradictory evidence.

(ii) *Spousal Privilege*

As noted earlier, a spouse is not competent nor compellable as a witness for the prosecution against a husband or a wife, except where the offence charged is one listed in section 4 of the Canada Evidence Act or is subject to the common law exception preserved by section 4(5) of that Act. The common law exception arises in those cases where the charge affects the person, health or liberty of the spouse of the accused. Unfortunately, the law is not entirely clear whether the charge itself must

---

9 Part I of the Constitution Act, 1982, being Schedule B of the Canada Act, 1982 (U.K.), 1982, c. 11.

specifically allege a threat to the spouse or if it is enough that the evidence itself discloses such a threat. In *D.P.P. v. Blady*,[10] the English Court of Criminal Appeal held that the nature of the charge must affect a spouse's health or liberty. However, recent Canadian cases have adopted a more liberal approach, allowing a spouse to testify where his or her health or liberty are affected.[11]

Although the common law exception extended to cases involving the health or liberty of a spouse, it did not, ironically, apply where the health or liberty of a child of the parties was involved. In other words, at common law, a wife was able to testify where her husband beat her but not where he beat their child. An attempt to rectify this situation was made in 1903 by an amendment to the Canada Evidence Act. That amendment listed a number of offences, primarily sexual offences, where a spouse was both competent and compellable to testify for the prosecution. However, the amendment omitted assaults. In 1983, that omission was corrected by a further amendment to section 4(4).

(iii) *Solicitor-Client Privilege*

What a person says to his lawyer in the latter's professional capacity and intended to be confidential is privileged. Neither the lawyer nor the client can be compelled to disclose the contents of that information. The basis of that rule is this: It is thought to be in the best interest of society as a whole that a person be allowed to consult with his legal adviser openly and freely, knowing that what he tells his legal adviser cannot be revealed. There is, however, one exception to this rule. It is not in the public interest that a person be allowed to consult with a lawyer in order to obtain advice on how to commit a crime. Such a communication is outside the scope of the rule and is not protected from being revealed by the solicitor.

It should be pointed out that the communication does not have to be given directly to the lawyer; it may be given to the lawyer's assistant or anyone acting under the lawyer's supervision. Moreover, even if a person changes lawyers, the information that he gave to his previous lawyer is still protected from disclosure. The protection also extends to information given by two or more persons to their lawyer in connection with the same matter.

The client, but not the lawyer, may waive a solicitor-client privilege. However, if he waives part of it, then he cannot claim protection for the

---

10 [1912] 2 K.B. 89 (C.A.).

11 *R. v. Sillars* (1978), 45 C.C.C. (2d) 283 (B.C. C.A.); *R. v. Czipps* (1979), 48 C.C.C. (2d) 166, 12 C.R. (3d) 193 (Ont. C.A.).

balance of the communication. If he waives any part of the privilege, he loses protection for the *entire* communication.

(iv) *Identity of Informers*

Law enforcement officers often depend upon professional informers to furnish them with information about criminal activities. The law therefore recognizes that it is in the best interest of society as a whole that people with important information about the commission of a crime be encouraged to come forward and give that information to the police without fear of disclosure. The law thus protects a witness for the Crown from answering questions that would have the effect of disclosing the identity of the informer.

This protection is, however, not absolute. If the court is persuaded that the identity of the informant would be material to demonstrate the innocence of the accused, then the court may order the witness to disclose the informant's identity.[12] For example, section 7 of the Canadian Charter of Rights and Freedoms ensures that everyone has the right "to life, liberty and security of the person and the right not to be deprived thereof except in accordance with the principles of fundamental justice." The principles of fundamental justice entitle everyone accused of a crime to make "full answer and defence." An example of where this occurred was the case of *R. v. Hunter.*[13] In that case, the defence sought to attack a search warrant that had been used to search the accused's residence where narcotics were discovered. It was held that, in the circumstances of that case, disclosure of the identity of the informer was crucial to the defence. The Crown was given the option of either disclosing the informant's identity, proceeding on a warrantless search, or withdrawing the prosecution.

(v) *Public Interest Privilege*

The law recognizes that it is not in the public interest to disclose certain information regarding governmental activities. At the same time, it is also recognized that for the administration of justice to operate properly, all litigants should have access to all evidence that may be of assistance to the fair disposition of issues arising in litigation. What the court must try to do is to balance these two competing interests. It will depend, as one judge has said, on "changing social conditions and the role of the government in society at various time."[14]

---

12 *Bisaillon c. Keable* (1983), 7 C.C.C. (3d) 385, 37 C.R. (3d) 289 (S.C.C.).

13 (1987), 34 C.C.C. (3d) 14, 57 C.R. (3d) 1 (Ont. C.A.).

14 *Carey v. R.* (1986), 30 C.C.C. (3d) 498 at 506-507 (S.C.C.), *per* LaForest J.

(vi) *Other Privileges*

The common law recognizes two other instances where persons may be protected from disclosing information. The first involves deliberations carried out by jurors in the jury room. No juror may be required to divulge what was said by any juror during deliberations. Not only is a juror protected from being compelled to disclose that information, he is guilty of contempt of court if he does so. Moreover, the Criminal Code now makes it an offence for a juror to disclose such information. The reason for this rule is straightforward. Verdicts are intended to be final and jurors should not be required to explain why they reached a particular verdict. If a juror was required to disclose what took place, it would encourage dissatisfied litigants from using every means to find out what went on in the jury room, in an effort to show that the result arrived at was not according to law. This would be contrary to public policy.

Finally, diplomats are protected from disclosure of information. This common law rule is based on the theory that courts have no jurisdiction over foreign subjects and that they should respect representatives of the government of another country. Such immunity, however, is not absolute where the safety of the country is imperiled.

(vii) *No Privilege*

There is a misconception by the public generally that persons such as doctors, psychiatrists, priests and journalists have the right to refuse to divulge information given to them by patients, penitents and informants. No such privilege exists. Nevertheless, some judges are loath to compel such witnesses to disclose information given in confidence to them; other judges have ordered the information to be disclosed but have refused to impose any penalty or have imposed a nominal one for the refusal to do so.

3. DOCUMENTARY EVIDENCE

(a) Generally

Direct or circumstantial evidence of a fact in issue may also be proved by a document. In order to prove the authenticity of a document, it is usually necessary to call as a witness the person who made it so that he can identify it. However, proof as to authorship can also be established by circumstantial evidence such as the finding of the document in the possession of someone, an admission of ownership or authorship, or testimony given by a handwriting expert. In such instance, it is still necessary for a witness to be asked to identify the document and to give evidence that will connect it with the fact in issue.

Let us assume for example that the accused is charged with forging a cheque. If someone is able to testify that he saw the accused writing out the cheque and can identify the particular document, that is direct evidence from which a judge or jury can conclude that the accused committed the crime. Let us assume, on the other hand, that no one saw him write the cheque but a witness is familiar with his handwriting. If the witness is able to identify the writing and signature in the cheque as belonging to the accused, that will not be direct evidence that the accused forged the cheque, but it will be circumstantial evidence from which a judge or jury can draw that inference.

Quite often, however, a document may be found in the possession of the accused which is incriminating in nature but no one is able to say that they saw the accused prepare it and no one can identify his signature. Let us assume, for example, that the accused, a butcher, is charged with selling horse meat which he fraudulently represented as beef. Assume that the police execute a search warrant at his home and find invoices from a horse rancher in Texas which indicate that certain horses were sold to the accused on a certain date. It is obvious that these invoices are relevant to the issue of whether the accused has been buying horses and selling them as beef. However, there is also the possibility that the documents are not relevant to the prosecution at all and simply indicate that the accused purchased some horses that he may still own or that he may have sold intact to someone else. It is also possible that the documents were fabricated by someone who wishes to harm the accused. Nevertheless, the courts have held that all documents found in the possession of an accused which are relevant to an issue before the court are admissible against him and may be considered by the judge and jury on the issue of his guilt. However, whether or not much weight should be attached to those documents will depend upon all of the circumstances of the case.

(b) Best Evidence Rule

The "best evidence" rule is a rule of evidence that requires the side that relies upon a document to produce the original unless the original was destroyed or cannot be found, or it is impossible or impractical to produce it. For example, it may be impossible or impractical to produce the original document if it is in the possession of someone in another country and a Canadian court has no jurisdiction to order its production.

The rule dates back to the very early common law when witnesses did not testify before juries. It was connected with the doctrine of "profert" in pleading, which required a party relying upon a document as a ground of action or defence, to produce it bodily to the court. As the law developed and witnesses were allowed to testify, the rule was justified on the basis that it prevented fraud, because it was presumed that if the original document existed, then it was likely being withheld for some sinister purpose. As well, there was a concern that a copy of a document, made by hand in those days, might be inaccurate.

Today, with modern photocopier machines, it is often possible to produce a document that cannot be distinguished from the original and the best evidence rule is often relaxed. On the other hand, the same technology allows production of an authentic-looking "copy" that may actually be a forgery made up of several documents pasted together. Nevertheless, lawyers will frequently admit that a particular document is a photocopy of the original and that it will not be necessary to comply with the best evidence rule. However, if the opposing side is not prepared to agree with the production of a photocopy or a copy, then the witness through whom the document is introduced must give some explanation as to why the original cannot be produced and, at least, be able to say that the copy is an exact reproduction of the original. In such instance, the court will generally admit it, and the issue as to whether it is an exact copy of the original will go to the question of the weight of the evidence but not to its admissibility.

4. ARTICLES AND THINGS

Another form of evidence, in addition to oral and documentary evidence, may be an article or a thing which is connected with the crime, such as a gun or a knife, or in the case of a stolen article, the article itself. This is known as "real evidence" because it can be seen, touched, heard or tested by the judge and jury. It is generally necessary, where such evidence is being tendered, for a witness to identify it and explain why it is being produced. It will then be made an exhibit (just as a document will be made an exhibit) so that if the verdict is appealed, the Court of Appeal will be able to determine what went on at the trial.

There may be circumstances where it may be impossible or inconvenient to produce the original article. For example, it would hardly add to the decorum of a trial to produce a stolen cow for inspection by the judge and jury, nor would it be practical to produce a stolen automobile. The usual practice is for a photograph to be taken of the particular article and to introduce the photograph in its place. Unless the other side agrees that the photograph is an exact replica of the article, then here again a witness must be called to testify that he took the photograph of the article or that he is familiar with it, and the photograph is an accurate photograph of it.

5. DEMONSTRATIVE EVIDENCE

Visual aids such as photographs or maps will often be admitted by the judge to assist the judge and jury in reaching their verdict. Obviously, whether the photograph, diagram or map, or any other item, will assist the judge and jury will often depend on the facts of the particular case.

Sometimes an opposing counsel will object to the introduction of a diagram or a map because it is not drawn to scale. In each case, the question of whether it should be admitted will depend on the judge, who must decide if it will assist him and the jury. If it is so distorted that it gives a wrong or a misleading impression, then he will undoubtedly refuse to admit it.

The most difficult question arises in the case of photographs. The first thing that must be established by the side that wishes to introduce a photograph is that it is an accurate depiction of the scene or the subject of the photograph, and that it is being offered to assist the trier in determining the issue before him. Often the main objection will be that the photograph, particularly of a victim, may inflame the jury and divert them from their main task, or cause them to be prejudiced against the accused. The judge has a discretion to exclude photographs if they are of minor assistance and their prejudicial effect far outweighs their assistance. On the other hand, the corollary of this is that if the photograph will assist the judge and jury in reaching their verdict, it will generally be admitted even if it is inflammatory. In each case, the judge must use his discretion to ensure that the accused receives a fair trial.[15]

---

15 *R. v. Kendall* (1988), 35 C.C.C. (3d) 105, 57 C.R. (3d) 249 (Ont. C.A.).

PART II

Excluded Evidence

3

Hearsay

1. THE RULE

Probably no rule of evidence is more misunderstood than the rule against hearsay. It is misunderstood because it is commonly believed that a witness may not testify as to what he was told by someone else. Because this is only a partial explanation of the rule, it is important then to start at the beginning.

The first thing we must ask ourselves whenever the possibility of hearsay arises is, "What are we seeking to prove?" For example, let us assume the accused is charged with robbing a bank at five minutes after 12:00 noon and X saw the accused enter the bank at 12:00 noon. Such evidence is offered not as direct evidence that the accused robbed the bank, but rather as circumstantial evidence from which a jury can infer that he was in the bank at the time of the robbery. Together with other evidence, it may establish that he was the robber. The rule is that only X may be called to testify that he saw the accused enter the bank at 12:00 noon.

Let us assume, however, that X is unavailable to testify but told Y that he saw the accused enter the bank at 12:00 noon. If the Crown seeks to introduce what X saw through the testimony of Y, that would be hearsay. Y will not be permitted to testify what X told him to prove that the accused entered the bank at 12:00 noon.

Why do we prohibit hearsay evidence? The fact that X saw the accused enter the bank at 12:00 noon is undoubtedly relevant to one of the three issues that the Crown must prove and is obviously logically probative. The answer is simply this. How can anyone cross-examine Y about what X told him? All Y can do is go on repeating what X told him. There is no way of testing whether X was telling the truth when he told Y that he saw the accused going into the bank at 12:00 noon. Unless X is compelled to come to court where his demeanour can be observed and his evidence tested by cross-examination, there is no way of ensuring that his story is true. Moreover, everyone knows that when information is passed from one person to the next, there is the risk that it may be misunderstood. Our system of justice recognizes that someone's life or liberty should not depend upon second-hand information.

Let us assume, however, that X also told Z that he saw the accused enter the bank at 2:00 p.m. and the defence wishes to call Z to say exactly what X told him. Is it hearsay? We must ask ourselves, "What does the evidence show?" The defence wishes to call the evidence to show that X should not be believed about having seen the accused enter the bank at 12:00 noon because he told Z that he saw him enter the bank at 2:00 p.m. It is not offered to prove that the accused entered the bank at 2:00 p.m., but to show that X was mistaken when he said to Y that he entered the bank at 12:00 noon. In such instance, it will be admitted because it does not offend the hearsay rule. It is original or first-hand evidence.

What the law of evidence seeks to ensure is that only original or first-hand evidence will be admitted to prove a fact in issue. Second-hand evidence will not suffice. On the other hand, where the fact in issue is whether something was said by someone else, then it will be admitted because it bears directly on the issue to be proved. It is original evidence — not second-hand evidence.

2. WHEN IS HEARSAY ALLOWED?

Most legal historians believe that the hearsay rule, like all exclusionary rules, owes its origin to the jury system. The jury was allowed to hear only evidence which was given under oath and subject to cross-examination. Some scholars argue that these two reasons have little substance today. For example, a witness who feels that his moral conscience cannot be bound by the oath is permitted to testify by affirmation. Moreover, juries today are sophisticated enough to know that the mere fact that a person takes an oath does not ensure the truth of his testimony. If anything does promote truth, it is the fear of prosecution for perjury.

The real reason why hearsay is still excluded today is because it cannot be tested by cross-examination. The law requires the person who has first-hand knowledge of the facts to come forward and to testify so that his evidence can be subjected to the scrutiny of cross-examination.

But what if that person is dead or otherwise unavailable to testify? Should the law, confronted with a choice of either accepting second-hand evidence or no evidence at all, choose the latter? No sooner was the exclusionary rule of hearsay invented in the late seventeenth century than judges began to realize that unless certain types of hearsay were admitted, serious crimes might go unpunished or litigants denied justice.

Professor Wigmore explained the exceptions in this way:

> The purpose and reason of the hearsay rule is the key to the exceptions to it. The theory of the hearsay rule is that many possible sources of inaccuracy and untrustworthiness which may lie underneath the bare untested assertion of a witness can best be brought to light and exposed, if they exist, by the test of cross-examination. But this test or security may in a given instance be superfluous; it may be sufficiently clear, in that instance, that the statement offered is free enough from the risk of inaccuracy and untrustworthiness, so that the test of cross-examination would be a work of supererogation. Moreover, the test may be impossible of employment — for example, by reason of the death of the declarant — so that, if his testimony is to be used at all, there is a necessity for taking it in the untested shape.[1]

3. EXCEPTIONS TO THE HEARSAY RULE

(a) Assertions of Deceased Persons

(i) *Dying Declarations*

Should a victim of a homicide be allowed to identify his killer before he died? A strict application of the hearsay rule would say no. However, if such evidence was not admitted, a murderer might escape punishment for his crime. On the other hand, there is always the concern that a person who is dying might try to settle a score with an enemy by falsely accusing him of murder. Faced with these two policy considerations, the courts decided to opt in favour of admitting the evidence for what it was worth. It was argued that anyone going to his maker was unlikely to perjure his soul by dying with a lie on his lips. At the same time, the courts were anxious to ensure that there would be no danger of mistake or an attempt

---

1 John H. Wigmore, *Wigmore On Evidence*, 3rd ed., Vol. 5 (Boston: Little, Brown and Co., 1974) para. 1420, at p. 251.

to settle old scores.[2] They did this by creating two conditions which must be met before such evidence would be admitted.

The first condition was that such evidence could only be allowed in a trial for the murder or manslaughter of the victim who made the declaration. In one case, the court refused to accept the dying declaration of a woman on the trial of a person charged with procuring her abortion, even though it resulted in her death. The other condition was that the victim must have had a settled, hopeless expectation of impending death at the time that he made the declaration. It was believed that his apprehension of death when the statement was made would ensure its trustworthiness, because a person is unlikely to tell a deliberate lie when he knows that he is dying and has no hope of recovery.

Obviously, such a limitation is often difficult to prove because it cannot always be assumed that a person who is dying knows that he is dying. Moreover, it is unlikely that even the most seriously injured person can appreciate that his life is in danger or that he will be told this by anyone who comes to his aid. Indeed, it is more likely that he will be encouraged to "hang on" until help comes.

Nevertheless, the rule has been and continues to be strictly applied. A famous example is the *Bedingfield* case.[3] Bedingfield was charged with the murder of a woman by cutting her throat. At the trial, a prosecution witness testified that she saw the victim running out of the house in which she had just been with Bedingfield. Her throat was almost completely severed. Just before the victim died, she said, "Look what Bedingfield has done to me." However, Cockburn C.J. refused to permit the witness to repeat what she heard the victim say. The fact that the wound itself was very serious was not enough for the court to draw the inference that the victim knew that she was dying. Fortunately, Bedingfield was convicted on other evidence.

Not only are restrictive conditions imposed on the admissibility of dying declarations, but courts also impose restrictions on what may be said if the declaration is admitted. The general rule is that the dying declaration must be confined to the circumstances that led to the victim's death. On the other hand, a dying declaration is not only admissible *against* an accused, it is also admissible in his favour. It is important therefore that everything that occurred immediately before and after the incident be allowed into evidence. Nevertheless, the court will impose certain restrictions. For example, in *R. v. Buck*,[4] the accused was charged with manslaughter arising out of an illegal operation on a young girl. Although

---

2 *Schwartzenhauer v. R.* (1935), 64 C.C.C. 1 (S.C.C.).

3 *R. v. Bedingfield* (1879), 14 Cox C.C. 341.

4 (1940), 74 C.C.C. 314 (Ont. C.A.).

the Court was prepared to allow a dying declaration as to what occurred at the time of the operation, it did not permit that part of her declaration which said that he attempted to procure an abortion on her some weeks before.

(ii) *Declarations Made in the Course of Duty*

This exception to the hearsay rule allows the use of an oral or written record or statement made by a deceased person in the usual and ordinary course of his business. The theory here is that if an agent or servant routinely does something, it is likely to be accurate. Moreover, it is argued that an agent or servant has an interest in making an accurate record because his employer will probably keep a check on its accuracy and fire him if it is not accurate.

One might seriously question whether these reasons are good enough to support this exception to the hearsay rule. We all know that people do make errors when they are making reports, and there is no way of checking the accuracy of the record once it is admitted. There is also the possibility that an employee may be trying to cheat or defraud his employer. In such case, an innocent accused may discover that he has no way of attacking the record's accuracy. However, error or deliberate fraud are considered to be such rare occurrences in comparison to usual conduct that it is felt to be in the public interest generally that the evidence be admitted.

Let us assume that Detective Jones sends out Officer Smith to make certain observations as to what is happening at the home of a suspect and to report back to him. In due course, Officer Smith returns and reports his observations to Detective Jones. If Officer Smith dies before the case comes to trial, then what he observed and reported to Detective Jones may be repeated by him in court because it was a report made in the usual and ordinary course of business. It is expected to be truthful and accurate because Jones would have checked its accuracy.

Let me give you another example. It is well-known that police officers, when conducting an investigation, make notes of everything that they observe to enable them to refresh their memories when called upon to testify days, weeks, months, or even years after the event. Obviously, an officer will try to be as accurate and as comprehensive as he can be in the preparation of notes that he will use to assist him when that time comes. Should such notes be admitted in evidence if the police officer dies before the trial of the accused? It is arguable that the notes are made in the usual and ordinary course of business. However, the notes are for the officer's personal use. Unless he is required to file those notes with a superior officer who can check their accuracy, it cannot be said that it is unlikely that the notes will be false or inaccurate.

The common law exception must be distinguished from the provisions of sections 29 and 30 of the Canada Evidence Act.[5] Those sections permit any financial record (section 29) or business record (section 30) made in the usual or ordinary course of business to be admitted, whether the person making them is dead or alive. A typical example involves a person's bank records. Let us assume that Mr. Smith purchased a television set with a cheque that was returned N.S.F. and was charged with either false pretences or fraud. To establish that Mr. Smith had insufficient funds in his account and that in the course of his dealing with the bank never did put in sufficient monies to honour the cheque, the prosecution would have to produce his bank records. The bank records themselves are hearsay. They are merely notations or records made by bank employees who dealt with Smith. Normally, the prosecution would be required to call every employee of the bank who ever dealt with Smith to show what he deposited in his account or withdrew from it.

Section 29 of the Canada Evidence Act allows the prosecution to introduce the record itself if it is established that at the time of making the entry, the record was one of the ordinary records of the bank, that the entry was made in the usual and ordinary course of business, that the record was in the custody or control of the bank, and that the copy is a true copy of the entry. Proof may be given by the manager or accountant of the bank, either orally or by affidavit. Section 30 permits the introduction of a business record made in the usual and ordinary course of business, provided that seven days notice is given before its production.[6]

(iii) Declarations Against Interest

Another exception to the hearsay rule is a declaration against penal, pecuniary or proprietary interest. In other words, if someone says something which might affect his liberty, his pocketbook, or his right or interest to certain property, what he says will be admitted in evidence if that person dies before he can be called upon to give evidence at trial. The rule was not always that way. For a long time, only declarations affecting a person's pecuniary or proprietary interest, but not his penal interest, were admissible in court.[7] However, in 1977, the Supreme Court of Canada decided in *R. v. O'Brien*[8] that it was only logical and proper that it should also extend to a penal interest. There Mr. Justice Dickson wrote:

The effect of the rule in *The Sussex Peerage Case*, as it has been generally

---

5 R.S.C. 1985, c. C-5.

6 *R. v. Bicknell* (1988), 41 C.C.C. (3d) 545 (B.C. C.A.).

7 *Sussex Peerage Case* (1844), 8 E.R. 1034 (H.L.).

8 (1977), 35 C.C.C. (2d) 209 (S.C.C.).

understood, is to render admissible the statement by a deceased that he had received payment of a debt from another or that he held a parcel of land as a tenant and not as owner, but to render inadmissible a confession by a deceased that he and not someone else was the real perpetrator of the crime. The distinction is arbitrary and tenuous. There is little or no reason why declarations against penal interest and those against pecuniary or proprietary interest should not stand on the same footing. A person is as likely to speak the truth in a matter affecting his liberty as in a matter affecting his pocketbook. For these reasons and the ever-present possibility that a rule of absolute prohibition could lead to grave injustice I would hold that, in a proper case, a declaration against penal interest is admissible according to the law of Canada; the rule as to absolute exclusion of declarations against penal interest, established in *The Sussex Peerage* case, should not be followed.[9]

In the same year, the Supreme Court of Canada also endorsed the following test for determining what was a declaration against penal interest:[10]

1. The declaration must be made to a person in such circumstances that the declarant could be said to apprehend being vulnerable to penal consequences. For example, if one says something to a member of the family, such as a parent or a spouse, or even a child, one does not expect that person to report him to the police and expose him to the risk of prosecution.
2. The declarant's vulnerability to penal consequences must not be too remote. In other words, one must be able to say that the person who hears the declaration will probably inform the police and expose the declarant to prosecution.
3. Not every declaration which appears to be against penal interest will be admitted. The court must look at the totality of the words spoken and conclude that the whole tenor of the weight is against the declarant's penal interest.
4. In a doubtful case, the court must look at all of the circumstances and consider whether or not there is any other evidence connecting the declarant with the crime, and whether there is evidence connecting the declarant and the accused.

It is of significance to note that the Court went so far as to say that the exception was not restricted only to declarants since deceased. The declaration was admissible if the declarant was unavailable to testify by reason of death, insanity, or grave illness which prevented the giving of testimony even from a bed, or absence in a jurisdiction where he could not be compelled by an order of the court to attend the accused's trial.

One can easily understand why the courts carefully scrutinize dec-

---

9 *Ibid.*, at 214.
10 *Demeter v. R.* (1977), 34 C.C.C. (2d) 137, 38 C.R.N.S. 317 (S.C.C.).

larations against penal interest. Just as a person who is about to die may wish to settle an old score with an enemy by accusing him of a crime, a person about to die may wish to save a member of his family or a friend from prosecution by falsely confessing to the crime. The law does not accept the former as evidence unless it is a dying declaration. The latter is accepted because the consequences are less severe. The possibility of convicting an innocent man based on a false accusation of guilt is far worse than the acquittal of a person who might be guilty.

(iv) *Declarations as to Physical and Mental Condition*

As was pointed out initially in this chapter, a statement is hearsay and is excluded only when it is offered to prove a fact in issue. If, however, the statement is offered only to prove that the statement was made, it is not hearsay and is clearly admissible. This is what is known as original evidence. The failure to understand the difference between hearsay and original evidence is a problem which frequently arises when one side seeks to call evidence of a statement or declaration made with respect to a physical or mental condition.

Let us take, for example, the decision of the Privy Council in *Ratten v. R.*[11] Ratten was charged with the murder of his wife by deliberately shooting her. His defence was that he shot her accidentally. Shortly before her death, Mrs. Ratten made a telephone call and said, "Get me the police, please." Mr. Ratten denied that his wife ever made a telephone call. The trial judge permitted the telephone operator who had received the call to say that she had received a telephone call, that the voice on the other end was hysterical and sobbing, and what the person said. It was held by the Privy Council that the evidence was relevant to prove the state of mind or emotion of Mrs. Ratten and to rebut the defence of accident.

In a Canadian case, *R. v. Wysochan*,[12] the issue was whether a woman was killed by her husband or by the accused. Each blamed the other. About half an hour after the woman had been shot, her husband appeared on the scene and she stretched out her arms to him and said, "Stanley, help me out because there is a bullet in my body" and later, "Stanley, help me. I am too hot." The Crown applied to have what she said admitted into evidence. The trial judge admitted her statements to show her state of mind. As he put it, "Would it not have been a most improbable thing had he been the author of her death that night?"

One might ask, "What was the relevance of the statements in both cases?" In the *Ratten* case, the fact that the victim wanted the police was

---

11 [1972] A.C. 378 (P.C.).

12 (1930), 54 C.C.C. 172 (Sask. C.A.).

not relevant to the question of who killed her. Similarly, in *Wysochan*, the fact that the victim wanted her husband to help her or that she was too hot was not relevant as to who shot her. The issue to be proved in each case was that the accused was the killer. If the victim had named her killer, then that statement would have been clearly hearsay and excluded unless it fell within one of the exceptions, such as a dying declaration or the *res gestae* (which will be discussed later). In both cases, the Court held that it fell into neither exception.

However, each statement was admitted because it was a declaration as to the victim's physical or mental condition, even though her physical or mental condition was not a fact which the Crown was required to prove to establish its case against the accused. What the Crown had to establish was that a murder had been committed, that the accused had committed it, and that he had the requisite mental intent. Because the victim's statement concerned her physical and mental condition, the Court said that it was not hearsay; rather, it was original evidence. Surprisingly, what the Court allowed the prosecution to do in each case was to have the statements admitted as original evidence and then use them for their hearsay content, that is, in *Ratten*, to show that the killing was deliberate and in *Wysochan*, to show that the accused and not the victim's husband committed the murder.

(b) Some Assertions of Living Persons

Although, traditionally, exceptions to the hearsay rule have only been allowed where the speaker is dead and therefore unable to testify, some recent decisions have gone so far as to suggest that declarations against interest or in the usual and ordinary course of duty will be admitted if the witness is unable, for some good reason, to come to the court to testify. One decision discussed earlier is *R. v. O'Brien*, where Chief Justice Dickson of the Supreme Court of Canada suggested that declarations against penal interest may be admitted where the declarant is unavailable by reason of death, insanity, grave illness, or absence from the jurisdiction of Canadian courts.

Probably the most controversial decision dealing with declarations made in the course of duty is *Ares v. Venner*,[13] arising out of Alberta. In that case, the plaintiff sued a doctor for not removing a cast from his leg in time. The issue before the Court was whether records kept by nurses at the hospital were admissible to show their observations of the pulse, temperature and condition of the plaintiff. Alberta, at that time, had no provision similar to that of other provinces such as Ontario which

---

13 [1970] S.C.R. 608, 12 C.R.N.S. 349.

authorized the admission of medical records of a patient. Although the nurses who made the records were alive and were, in fact, waiting outside the courtroom to testify, the Supreme Court of Canada held that such records were still admissible as declarations made in the ordinary course of duty and were "*prima facie* proof of the facts stated therein."

In reaching that conclusion, the Court rejected the decision of the House of Lords in *Myers v. D.P.P,*[14] where it was held that judges should not re-state the law to meet modern conditions but should leave it to Parliament to do the job. Ironically, it was not really necessary for the Supreme Court to have extended the rule at all. The issue in *Ares v. Venner* was whether the doctor was negligent in failing to remove the cast from the plaintiff's leg after he read the nurses' notes which described the plaintiff's condition (*i.e.*, that his toes were swollen, numb, blue etc.), not whether the contents of the notes were correct. In other words, had the nurses' notes been admitted, not as proof of the contents, but to show that the doctor should have been alerted by what he read in those notes to look at the plaintiff's leg, no hearsay problem would have arisen.

(c) *Res Gestae*

The term "*res gestae*" is a Latin phrase that is too often used and misused by judges and lawyers. Professor Wigmore called it useless "because every rule of Evidence to which it has ever been applied exists as a part of some other well established principle and can be explained in the terms of that principle." He also called it harmful "because by its ambiguity it invites the confusion of one rule with another and thus creates uncertainty as to the limitations of both." He suggested that it should be wholly repudiated. Regrettably, judges and lawyers continue to use it more than ever.

The rule has been expressed this way:

> Acts, declarations, and incidents which constitute, or accompany and explain, the fact or transaction in issue, are admissible, for or against either party, as forming part of the *res gestae*.[15]

In *Teper v. R.,*[16] Lord Normand attempted to justify the reception of evidence which forms part of the *res gestae* this way:

> It appears to rest ultimately on two propositions, that human utterance is both a fact and a means of communication, and that human action may be so interwoven with words that the significance of the action cannot be

---

14 [1964] 2 All E.R. 881 (H.L.).
15 *Phipson on Evidence* (11th ed.), para. 171.
16 [1952] A.C. 480 (P.C.).

understood without the correlative words, and the dissociation of the words from the action would impede the discovery of truth.[17]

The above passages speak of *res gestae* as being words which give significance to or explain conduct or action. In *R. v. Bedingfield*, discussed earlier, the victim, who was Bedingfield's mistress, came out of a room where Bedingfield was subsequently found, pointed to her throat which was cut, and said to one of her assistants, "See what Harry has done." She died ten minutes later. Bedingfield's first name was Harry. The trial judge, Chief Justice Cockburn, would not permit the statement to be admitted in evidence because the transaction, that is the cutting of her throat, was over and completed when she made the statement. Later decisions accepted this restriction and argued that a statement or declaration could not be admitted as part of the *res gestae* unless it accompanied the act and explained it.

Professor Wigmore strongly criticized this restriction. He argued that it arose out of a failure to understand the distinction between what may be described as a verbal act and a spontaneous exclamation. A verbal act is simply words which accompany an act and which explain it. As Professor Wigmore pointed out:

> Without the words, the act as a whole may be incomplete; and until the words are taken into consideration, the desired significance cannot be attributed to the wordless conduct.[18]

Without the accompanying words, the act has no significance. The words explain the act. This means that when a witness, who has seen the act and heard the accompanying words, testifies as to what he has seen and heard, he is giving not second-hand evidence but first-hand or original evidence. In other words, it is not an exception to the hearsay rule because it is not hearsay at all. This means that *res gestae* is not, in a strict sense, an exception to the hearsay rule. It allows the admission of statements which would otherwise be hearsay to explain conduct or actions which might otherwise be ambiguous.

Professor Wigmore, however, has argued that spontaneous exclamations ought to be admitted as exceptions to the hearsay rule. His reasons are these:

> Under certain external circumstances of physical shock, a stress of nervous excitement may be produced which stills the reflective faculties and removes their control, so that the utterance which then occurs is a spontaneous and sincere response to the actual sensations and perceptions already produced by the external shock. Since this utterance is made under the immediate and

---

17 *Ibid.*, at 486.
18 *Supra*, note 1, Vol. 6, para. 1772, at p. 267.

uncontrolled domination of the senses, and during the brief period when considerations of self-interest could not have been brought fully to bear by reasoned reflection, the utterance may be taken as particularly trustworthy, (or at least as lacking the usual grounds of untrustworthiness), and thus as expressing the real tenor of the speaker's belief as to the facts just observed by him; and may therefore be received as testimony to those facts.[19]

If we might use the *Bedingfield* case as an example, Professor Wigmore would argue that the exclamation of Bedingfield's mistress as to "what Harry has done" was "a spontaneous and sincere response to the actual sensations and perceptions already produced by the external shock" of having her throat cut. It was also made "during the brief period when considerations of self interest could not have been brought fully to bear by reasoned reflection." Thus, he would argue that the utterance should be taken as particularly trustworthy and should be admitted as an exception to the hearsay rule.

For almost seventy years, *Bedingfield* was religiously followed by Canadian and English courts. In 1950, there was some attempt to introduce the concept of "spontaneous exclamation" in an Ontario case but it was quickly rejected. In *R. v. Leland*,[20] the accused and her husband were jointly charged with manslaughter arising out of the stabbing of one, Monteith, in whose house both were residing as roomers. During a quarrel between Monteith and the accused's husband, all of the lights in the house were turned off. When the lights were turned on again, Monteith was heard to say to his wife, "Rose, she stabbed me" and he died a few minutes later. The victim's wife's name was Rose. The trial judge admitted the statement without specifically referring to it as a "spontaneous exclamation." However, the Ontario Court of Appeal said that he was wrong because "our rules of evidence do not seem to extend to cover a case of spontaneous exclamation, in the broad terms stated by Wigmore." Nor was the Court prepared to admit it as part of the *res gestae* because "the fight had ceased. No one was pursuing the deceased or seeking to continue the struggle."

Finally in 1972, in *Ratten v. R.* (discussed earlier), the House of Lords concluded that the *Bedingfield* rule was too restrictive. In *Ratten*, the Crown sought to introduce the evidence of a telephone operator who had received a telephone call from the deceased's home ten minutes before she was shot. The call came from a woman who sounded hysterical and who said, "Get me the police, please." She gave her address but before a connection was made, hung up. The trial judge admitted the statement, and Lord Wilberforce, delivering the judgment of the Privy Council, said that he

---

19 *Ibid.*, Vol. 6, para. 1747, at p. 195.
20 (1950), 98 C.C.C. 337 (Ont. C.A.).

was correct in doing so. In his view, the admissibility of such statements did not depend on there being exact contemporaneity with the act to be explained.

> ... hearsay evidence may be admitted if the statement providing it is made in such conditions (always being those of approximate but not exact contemporaneity) of involvement or pressure as to exclude the possibility of concoction or distortion to the advantage of the maker or the disadvantage of the accused.[21]

The test which the trial judge had to apply was whether there was the possibility of concoction or fabrication, not whether the statement was part of the event or transaction:

> ... if the drama, leading up to the climax, has commenced and assumed such intensity and pressure that the utterance can safely be regarded as a true reflection of what was unrolling or actually happening, it ought to be received.[22]

Ratten was re-affirmed 14 years later by the House of Lords in *R. v. Blastland*[23] and again, a year later, by the House of Lords in *R. v. Andrews (D.J.)*.[24] In *Andrews*, *Bedingfield* was specifically overruled.

Although Canadian courts have not yet embraced the concept of "spontaneous exclamation" espoused by Wigmore, there has been a relaxation of the narrow "exact contemporaneity" test of *Bedingfield*.[25] For example, in *R. v. Garlow*,[26] Van Camp J. admitted the statement of the deceased made shortly after the attack in response to the question of what had happened because there was no time to fabricate the story nor reason to do so. And in *R. v. Kahn*, Mr. Justice Robins wrote:

> The time that may elapse before a statement following an event capable of rendering it spontaneous is rendered inadmissible will depend on a variety of factors. These include, for instance, the nature and circumstances of the act or event, the nature and circumstances of the statement, the place where the event occurred or the statement was made, the possible influence of intervening events, and the condition and age of the declarant. Each case must depend on its own circumstances; no two cases are identical, and the exact length of time is not subject to mathematical measurement. In any given case, the ultimate question is whether the statement relating to the alleged startling event was made near enough in time to the event to exclude any realistic opportunity for fabrication or concoction.[27]

---

21 *Supra*, note 11 at 391.
22 *Ibid.*, at 389-390.
23 [1986] A.C. 41 (H.L.).
24 [1987] A.C. 281 (H.L.).
25 *R. v. Clark* (1983), 7 C.C.C. (3d) 46, 35 C.R. (2d) 357 (Ont. C.A.), leave to appeal to S.C.C. refused (1983), 7 C.C.C. (3d) 46n (S.C.C.).
26 (1976), 31 C.C.C. (2d) 163 (Ont. H.C.).
27 (1988), 42 C.C.C. (3d) 197 at 210, 64 C.R. (3d) 281 (Ont. C.A.).

4

Previous Consistent Statements

1. THE RULE

The general rule at common law is that a witness may not be asked in chief whether he or she previously made a statement consistent with his or her present testimony. For example, the prosecutor is not entitled to ask the victim of an assault whether he or she made a statement to the police consistent with his or her present testimony; nor may any other prosecution witness be permitted to repeat the victim's prior consistent statement. When it comes to the defence, there are two aspects of this rule. The first is that the defence is not allowed to call the accused or any other witness to testify that the accused made a statement before trial declaring his innocence. Second, the defence is not allowed to ask a prosecution witness during cross-examination about any statement made by the accused declaring his innocence.[1]

The rule, often called the "rule against self-serving evidence," explains one of the reasons for it. It is to prevent witnesses, particularly an accused, from manufacturing or inventing evidence which serves their own interests. It is only human nature for a jury to believe that because a victim previously

---

1 *R. v. Campbell* (1977), 38 C.C.C. (2d) 6, 1 C.R. (3d) 309 (Ont. C.A.).

declared the accused's guilt, or an accused protested his innocence before trial, that evidence must be true. The purpose of the rule is to prevent the jury from being swayed by this side issue.

A good example of the rule is the *R. v. Roberts*[2] case. Roberts was charged with the murder of his girlfriend. His defence was that he had shot her accidentally while they were making up after a quarrel. Two days after the shooting, he told his father that his defence was that the shooting had been an accident. His father was not permitted to give evidence of that conversation because it was self-serving.

Another reason for the rule, particularly where it affects the defence, is to prevent an accused from avoiding the witness box by having someone else advance his defence. If the accused wishes to tell his story of what happened, he may do so by entering the witness box where he will be required to testify under oath and be subject to cross-examination.

However, the rule will not apply where the prosecution chooses to make the accused's explanation part of its case. For example, if the Crown decides, for whatever reason, to introduce the accused's statement at trial, it will be admissible even if it is self-serving. It is only where the defence attempts to introduce such evidence that the rule steps in to prevent it.

2. EXCEPTIONS TO THE RULE

(a) To Rebut the Suggestion of Recent Fabrication

There are undoubtedly instances where prior consistent statements should be admitted. The first is where the prosecution suggests that the defence presented was recently invented or contrived. Here, it is only fair that the defence be allowed to rebut that suggestion by leading evidence that the accused's defence has been consistent throughout.[3]

As a practical matter, the question of recent fabrication will not arise frequently as a result of the right to remain silent. It would be very unfortunate if police officers were required to warn an accused of his right to remain silent and then be allowed to use that silence to complain of recent fabrication when the defence is revealed for the first time at trial. The exception will arise where the defence is one of alibi. Here, it is generally prudent for the defence to give the prosecution the particulars of that alibi at the earliest opportunity.[4]

---

2 (1942), 28 Cr. App. R. 102 (C.C.A.).

3 *R. v. Garofoli* (1988), 41 C.C.C. (3d) 97, 64 C.R. (3d) 193 (Ont. C.A.), leave to appeal to S.C.C. granted (1989), 103 N.R. 234n (S.C.C.).

4 *R. v. Robertson* (1975), 21 C.C.C. (2d) 385, 29 C.R.N.S. 141 (Ont. C.A.), leave to appeal to S.C.C. refused (1975), 21 C.C.C. (2d) 385n (S.C.C.).

(b) To Show Consistency of Identification

The rule is regularly breached in cases where the identification of the accused is in dispute. Evidence by a witness that the person standing in the prisoner's dock "is the man" is generally regarded as valueless because it is open to "honest mistake and self-deception."[5]

Therefore, if the prosecution is relying on eye-witness identification, the police will usually attempt, in the initial stages of the investigation, to have the witness view a series of photographs or attend a lineup. The purpose is to see if the witness is able to pick out, without any suggestion by the police, the suspected offender. When the matter goes to trial, the witness will then be able to testify that he was shown a series of photographs or attended a lineup and picked out the accused without prompting.

Where the witness does this, he is, in effect, giving evidence of his own prior consistent statement. Similarly, police officers present at the out of court identification are regularly allowed to testify that the witness viewed a series of photographs or attended a lineup and picked out the accused. When they do so, they are giving essentially hearsay evidence.

(c) As Part of the *Res Gestae*

Although *res gestae*, discussed earlier, is commonly linked with the hearsay rule, it is also an exception to the rule against previous consistent statements.

In *R. v. Graham*,[6] a majority panel of the Supreme Court of Canada held that the explanation given by an accused when first found in possession of stolen property was admissible as part of the *res gestae*. The rationale for this decision was that the explanation given at the moment of discovery, if the same as that given at trial, is strong proof of the consistency of the accused's evidence.

(d) To Rebut the Presumption of Consent in Sexual Assaults

At common law, the fact that a complaint was made by the victim of a sexual assault, but not what she actually said, was admissible at the trial of her attacker to show consistency in the victim's testimony. This rule developed from the ancient requirement that the victim of an attack should raise the hue and cry if a prosecution of rape was to succeed. It was based on the belief and presumption that a woman who did not complain of rape at the earliest opportunity must have consented to

---

5 *R. v. Browne and Angus* (1951), 99 C.C.C. 141, 11 C.R. 297 (B.C. C.A.).

6 (1972), 7 C.C.C. (2d) 93, 19 C.R.N.S. 117 (S.C.C.).

intercourse. The fact of the complaint, so long as it was made at the earliest opportunity, was admitted to show that the victim acted as one would normally expect her to do after a sexual attack. It allowed the judge and jury to infer that her consistency in repeating the same story at trial that she did after her attack was because she was a credible person.

Initially, the rule only allowed the fact of the complaint to be admitted but not what the victim actually said. Eventually, in *R. v. Lillyman*,[7] what the victim actually said was admitted, although the jurors were instructed that it was only relevant to show consistency in her conduct, presumably as a vain effort to avoid the rule against self-serving testimony.

Not surprisingly, this archaic rule was finally abrogated by Parliament in 1983. Its abolition does not mean that a complaint by a victim of a sexual assault is no longer admissible; it only means that there is no longer a presumption of consent which must be rebutted by evidence of a complaint. If there is no presumption of consent, then there is no necessity for the Crown to lead evidence of a complaint in chief. However, if the defence suggests that the victim consented, it would follow that the prosecution should be allowed to lead evidence of a complaint to show consistency in her conduct. At the same time, the defence should be permitted to bring out the particulars of the complaint where it appears that it is inconsistent with the complainant's testimony at trial.

---

7 [1896] 2 Q.B. 167 (C.C.R.).

5

Character Evidence

1. THE RULE

One of the most important rules of evidence is that the prosecution is generally not allowed to give evidence of an accused's bad character or previous convictions to show that he probably committed the offence charged. I say generally because section 360 of the Criminal Code has an unusual provision which allows the Crown, in prosecutions for possession of stolen property or stolen mail, to introduce evidence of an accused's convictions for theft or possession within the previous five years.

The general rule excluding character evidence is unique to the common law system of criminal justice. In many countries, evidence of an accused's character is not only admissible, it is the first to be adduced at his trial. Those countries believe that a man's previous history and conduct is relevant to the issue of whether he may be guilty of the charge he is now facing.

There is a great deal of merit in that view. As a matter of common sense, everyone of us takes into account the history and character of someone with whom we are dealing. The common law, however, rejects this view, not because it is not based on common sense, but because of a number of policy reasons. The first is the question of fairness. It is obviously more equitable to compel the prosecution to try a man on the facts of the particular case rather than on his whole life. The second is that since criminal cases are generally tried by juries, it is important that the jury be allowed to focus on the particular issues to be proved rather than to be sidetracked by what the accused may have done on other occasions. There is always the risk that jurors, who have no legal training or experience, may be too influenced by the accused's previous conduct and conclude that because of his previous criminal habits, he is probably guilty of the offence. As one judge has said, "The evidence is relevant to the issue, but is excluded for reasons of policy and humanity; because although by admitting it you may arrive at justice in one case out of a hundred, you would probably do injustice in the other ninety-nine."[1]

The general rule was stated by Lord Herschell L.C. in *Makin v. A.G. for New South Wales*:

> It is undoubtedly not competent for the prosecution to adduce evidence tending to show that the accused has been guilty of criminal acts other than those covered by the indictment, for the purpose of leading to the conclusion that the accused is a person likely from his criminal conduct or character to have committed the offence for which he is being tried. On the other hand, the mere fact that the evidence adduced tends to show the commission of other crimes does not render it inadmissible if it be relevant to an issue before the jury, and it may be so relevant if it bears upon the question whether the acts alleged to constitute the crime charged in the indictment were designed or accidental, or to rebut a defence which would otherwise be open to the accused. The statement of these general principles is easy, but it is obvious that it may often be very difficult to draw the line and to decide whether a particular piece of evidence is on one side or the other.[2]

2. EXCEPTIONS TO THE RULE

(a) When the Accused Puts His Character in Issue

Although the rule is that the Crown may not adduce evidence of bad character, that rule applies only to the prosecution. An accused is always entitled to introduce evidence of his own good character. Indeed, the fact that the accused may have lived a good and honest life to date may be the only defence that he has to the crime charged against him. He may lead evidence of his character in one of two ways.

First of all, he may go into the witness stand and swear not only that he did not commit the crime, but that he is also not the kind of person who would commit such a crime. Secondly, he is entitled to call witnesses to attest to his good character. These witnesses are not allowed to give their personal opinion of the accused's good character, nor to point out

---

1 *R. v. Rowton* (1865), Le & Ca. 520 at 541 (C.C.R.), *per* Willes J.

2 [1894] A.C. 57 at 65 (P.C.).

specific incidents of good character or citizenship, such as the fact that the accused may have saved the life of a child or returned a wallet that he found in the street (although this rule is not always strictly enforced). The rule is that the witness can only swear to the general reputation of the accused in the community and not give his or her personal opinion of him.

It is generally handled this way. The witness will be asked whether he or she knows the accused's reputation for honesty in the community (where the crime is one of dishonesty) or peacefulness (where the crime is one of violence), etc. If the answer is in the affirmative, he or she will then be asked, "What is that reputation?" and the witness will be allowed to give evidence of the community's view.

Once the accused puts his own character in issue, it is only fair that the prosecution should have the right to answer that evidence by calling evidence of bad character. Evidence of bad character may be led in the form of witnesses who disagree with the character witnesses for the accused and wish to testify as to the accused's bad reputation in the community. Their evidence will be led in the same fashion as that of the defence witnesses. Evidence of bad character may also be led in the form of previous convictions. Section 593 of the Criminal Code authorizes the prosecution to introduce evidence of previous convictions in such instance. Section 667 of the Code sets out the method by which such previous convictions may be put to him (a matter that will be dealt with in a later section).

(b) Where the Accused Puts the Victim's Character in Issue

The general rule is that the character of the victim is not admissible on the issue of whether the accused committed the offence. Even "bad" people are entitled to protection from having crimes committed against them. However, there may be instances where the character of the victim may be relevant to the defence of the accused. For example, if the accused is charged with a crime of violence such as murder, manslaughter or assault, and his defence is self-defence, the disposition of the victim for violence is relevant to the issue of who was the aggressor.[3]

Evidence of the victim's propensity for aggression may be brought out through the cross-examination of Crown witnesses or by the defence calling evidence of the victim's general reputation for violence. In such instance, it is only fair that the prosecution be allowed, by way of reply, to establish that the accused has a propensity for violence and that it was he, not the victim, who was the aggressor.

In England, the accused may not be asked questions about his previous

---

3 *R. v. Scopelliti* (1981), 63 C.C.C. (2d) 481 (Ont. C.A.).

criminal convictions or questions tending to show previous bad character unless the accused puts his own character in issue or attacks the character of the Crown witnesses. The English rule is essentially a tit-for-tat rule. So long as the defence does not attack the prosecution, the prosecution is not entitled to attack the defence. This rule is contained in the Criminal Evidence Act of 1898.

Canada has no similar provision. The suggestion that a Crown witness may not be telling the truth does not give the prosecution, under Canadian law, the right to attack the accused by leading evidence of his bad character. The only recognized exception arises where the defence is one of self-defence. Here the Crown, as indicated earlier, is allowed to call evidence of the accused's propensity for aggression only in reply to the defence's suggestion that it was the victim who was the aggressor. On the other hand, once a witness enters the witness stand, whether he is the victim, the accused, or anyone else, he loses all protection. His credibility becomes relevant to the truth and accuracy of his testimony. In such instance, the witness may be cross-examined to show that he is of bad character and not worthy of belief.

(c) When the Accused Testifies

At common law, an accused was not allowed to give evidence in his own defence. This rule was based on the civil practice which prohibited persons from testifying in a case which affected their own interest. In Canada, the right of an accused to testify on his own behalf was recognized first in 1886 with respect to some offences, and finally in 1893 by the Canada Evidence Act with respect to all offences. Section 4(1) of the Canada Evidence Act[4] provides:

> 4(1) Every person charged with an offence, and, except as otherwise provided in this section, the wife or husband, as the case may be, of the person so charged is a competent witness for the defence whether the person so charged is charged solely or jointly with any other person.

This means that although an accused has the right to give evidence on his behalf, he cannot be forced to go into the witness box if he does not choose to do so.

An accused who chooses to testify on his own behalf is in the same position as any other witness. When he does, he puts himself forward as a credible person and that credibility is subject to attack by cross-examination, as any other witness would be. However, it has been recognized that the right of the Crown to attack the credibility of an accused

---

4 R.S.C. 1985, c. C-5.

is not superior to the policy rule which protects an accused against an attack upon his character. For that reason, while an accused, like an ordinary witness, is generally open to cross-examination at large as to credibility, he should not be cross-examined as to previous misconduct or discreditable associations for the purpose of attacking his credibility, unless such cross-examination is relevant to prove the falsity of his own evidence.[5]

The criminal record of a witness or the accused stands on a different level. Section 12(1) of the Canada Evidence Act provides:

> 12(1) A witness may be questioned as to whether he has been convicted of any offence, and on being so questioned, if he either denies the fact or refuses to answer, the opposite party may prove the conviction.

In England, section 1(f) of the Criminal Evidence Act, 1898 forbids cross-examination of an accused on his record unless it is relevant to a fact in issue, the accused leads evidence of his own good character or impugns the character of the prosecutor or his witness, or gives evidence against a co-accused. In Canada, there is no such protection. Section 12(1) of the Canada Evidence Act permits an accused to be cross-examined about his criminal record even if he does not attack the Crown witnesses nor lead evidence of his own good character.

For a long time, it was believed that a trial judge had a general discretion to exclude evidence of prior convictions where the revelation of those convictions would prejudice the accused in the eyes of the jury. However, four years before the enactment of the Canadian Charter of Rights and Freedoms, it was decided that a trial judge had no discretion to prevent the Crown from cross-examining the accused as to prior convictions for any offence.[6] Moreover, it was held that the words "any offence" in section 12(1) included convictions for offences outside of Canada, provided that the process of adjudication of guilt constituted a conviction under Canadian law. In an earlier case, it was also decided that a "conviction" included the sentence so that the accused could be cross-examined on the penalty imposed.[7]

However in 1988, the Supreme Court of Canada decided that section 12(1) was not so absolute in its terms. The Court ruled that a trial judge did have a discretion to exclude evidence of previous convictions in those cases where a mechanical application of section 12 would undermine the right to a fair trial as guaranteed by the Charter of Rights.[8]

---

5 *R. v. Davison* (1974), 20 C.C.C. (2d) 424 (Ont. C.A.), leave to appeal to S.C.C. refused (1974), 20 C.C.C. (2d) 424n (S.C.C.).

6 *R. v. Stratton* (1978), 42 C.C.C. (2d) 449, 3 C.R. (3d) 289 (Ont. C.A.).

7 *R. v. Boyce* (1974), 23 C.C.C. (2d) 16, 28 C.R.N.S. 336 (Ont. C.A.).

8 *R. v. Corbett* (1988), 41 C.C.C. (3d) 385, 64 C.R. (3d) 1 (S.C.C.).

(d) When the Evidence is of Similar Facts

At the outset of this chapter it was pointed out that although, as a matter of common sense, the character of an accused may be relevant to his guilt or innocence, such evidence is excluded because the law considers it unfair to allow the prosecution to try a man on his whole life rather than on the facts of the case. Another purpose is to ensure that the jury's attention is not diverted from the central issue in the case. On the other hand, there may be instances where evidence of bad character or disposition is so probative of the particular issues in the case that it should be admitted. As Lord Hershell L.C. pointed out in the second part of his classic statement of the rule in *Makin v. A.G. for New South Wales*:

> On the other hand, the mere fact that the evidence adduced tends to show the commission of other crimes does not render it inadmissible if it be relevant to an issue before the jury, and it *may be so relevant if it bears upon the question whether the acts alleged to constitute the crime charged in the indictment were designed or accidental, or to rebut a defence which would otherwise be open to the accused.* The statement of these general principles is easy, but it is obvious that it may often be very difficult to draw the line and to decide whether a particular piece of evidence is on the one side or the other.[9]

In the almost one hundred years which have passed since Lord Hershell's classic statement was delivered, judges, lawyers and legal scholars have attempted "to draw the line" in an effort to make some sense of the rule. The courts have approached the task by creating categories of relevance in an effort to place each case in a particular pigeon-hole. However, in 1975, the House of Lords in *Boardman v. D.P.P.*[10] decided that although the categories were useful illustrations of the similar fact rule, they were not an automatic ticket to admissibility. The Court said that the proper approach was for the trial judge to balance the probative value of the evidence against the prejudice which the accused might suffer if the evidence was admitted:

> The basic principle must be that the admission of similar fact evidence . . . is exceptional and requires a strong degree of probative force. This probative force is derived, if at all, from the circumstances that the facts testified to by the several witnesses bear to each other such a striking similarity that they must, when judged by experience and common sense, either all be true, or have arisen from a common cause to the witnesses or from pure coincidence. The jury may, therefore, properly be asked to judge whether the right conclusion is that all are true, so that each story is supported by the other.[11]

The approach recommended in *Boardman* has been accepted in

---

9 *Supra*, note 2 at 65.
10 (1975), 60 Cr. App. R. 165 (H.L.).
11 *Ibid.*, at 174-175, *per* Lord Wilberforce.

Canada. In a recent decision of the Supreme Court of Canada, *R. v. B. (C.R.)* (released April 12, 1990), McLachlin J., writing for the majority, added:

> The judge must consider such factors as the degree of distinctiveness or uniqueness between the similar fact evidence and the offences alleged against the accused, as well as the connection, if any, of the evidence to issues other than propensity, to the end of determining whether, in the context of the case before him, the probative value of the evidence outweighs its potential prejudice and justifies its reception.[12]

Although the prosecution is no longer required to show that the evidence falls into a particular category such as "to prove intent" or "to prove a system" or "to have a plan" or "to show malice" or "to rebut the defence of accident or mistake" or "to prove identity" or "to rebut the defence of innocent association," a few examples will illustrate the weighing process that a judge must go through.

In the famous "Brides in the Bath" case *(Smith)*,[13] Smith had married successively three women, all of whom had drowned, supposedly accidentally, in a bath that he had arranged to have installed. In each case, Smith benefited financially from their deaths. He was charged with the murder of his first wife and the prosecution was granted the right to call evidence as to the circumstances surrounding the deaths of his second and third wives. The English Court of Criminal Appeal held that the evidence was admissible to rebut the defence of accident. Although there was no evidence directly connecting Smith with the death of any of his wives, the Court held that it was highly unlikely that all three could have died by accident.

The trial judge, Scrutton J. charged the jury this way:

> If you find an accident which benefits a person and you find that the person has been sufficiently fortunate to have that accident happen to him a number of times, benefiting him each time, you draw a very strong, frequently and irresistible inference, that the occurrence of so many accidents benefiting him is such a coincidence that it can not have happened unless it was designed.[14]

The *Makin* case is another interesting example. Makin and his wife were charged with the murder of a child whose body had been found in their back garden. The Makins had agreed to look after the child and had received a very small amount of money from the child's mother. The bodies of eleven other infants who had been entrusted to their care for a very small amount of money were also found buried in the gardens of

---

12 (1990), 55 C.C.C. (3d) 1 (S.C.C.).
13 *R. v. Smith* (1915), 11 Cr. App. R. 229 (C.C.A.).
14 *Ibid.*, at 233.

houses occupied by the Makins at various times. Although no one had seen the Makins kill any of the children, it was held that such evidence was admissible to show that the children had died, not from natural causes or by accident, but by design. The evidence was tendered to show that the only natural or irresistible inference that the jury could draw was that the child had died by design and that it was the Makins who had killed him.

Both *Makin* and *Smith* are straightforward instances of the application of the similar fact evidence exception. In *Boardman*, the House of Lords suggested that similar fact evidence might be introduced where it was strikingly similar or had common unusual and highly distinctive features. An example given was the *Straffen*[15] case. Straffen was accused of the murder of a little girl who was found strangled. No attempt had been made to assault her sexually or to conceal her body, although it might easily have been done. Straffen, who had just escaped from Broadmoor and was in the neighbourhood at the time of the crime, had previously committed two murders of young girls. These murders had the same peculiar features. It was held that it would have been a most extraordinary coincidence if, while Straffen was temporarily at large, another madman in the same area had killed the little girl by strangulation and had neither assaulted her nor made any attempt to conceal her.

Although in some instances, such as the *Straffen* case, the distinctive features between the similar fact evidence and the offence charged will support the conclusion that the accused committed the offence, it is usually necessary for the Crown to lead evidence connecting the accused with the crime charged before similar fact evidence will be admitted. For example, in *Sweitzer v. R.*,[16] the accused was originally charged with fifteen counts of sexual assault on women but, before the trial began, the trial judge severed the various counts. The prosecution then elected to proceed on the first count and was permitted by the judge to lead evidence of the fourteen other assaults as similar fact evidence. However, the victims were unable to identify their assailant in eleven of those fifteen assaults, including the first count. There was some direct evidence identifying Sweitzer as the assailant in four assaults and there was some similarity between the conduct of the assailant in those four episodes with the conduct of the assailant in the eleven episodes where he could not be identified. It was held by Mr. Justice McIntyre of the Supreme Court of Canada that the trial judge erred in admitting evidence of the eleven episodes because they were not shown to be connected in any way with Sweitzer. He made no comment as to whether the four connected to Sweitzer were admissible

---

15 *R. v. Straffen* (1952), 36 Cr. App. R. 132 (C.C.A.).
16 (1982), 68 C.C.C. (2d) 193 (S.C.C.).

because a new trial was ordered. Nor did he indicate whether the eleven episodes would have been admissible if the prosecution had proceeded with one of the four incidents directly linked to Sweitzer and had applied for leave to lead evidence of the eleven unconnected offences on the basis of striking similarity.

Although the *Boardman* case talked about the necessity for similar fact evidence to be strikingly similar, it has been held that there may be instances where similar fact evidence may be admissible even though it is not strikingly similar. An example is *R. v. Carpenter (No. 2),*[17] an arson case. Carpenter was the owner of property destroyed in a fire. He was the beneficiary of a fire insurance policy. There was evidence that he had been on the premises a few hours before the fire occurred. The trial judge had excluded evidence of two other fires within a six month period at the premises because the evidence as to the fires was not strikingly similar. The Ontario Court of Appeal held that he was wrong. Evidence of striking similarity with respect to fires was not required where the defence raised was that of accident. That same court has also held that evidence of striking similarity is not necessary where the evidence is tendered to prove a state of mind, knowledge, intent, authority or system.[18]

One area that has caused difficulty is where the accused is a member of an abnormal group with the same propensities as the perpetrator of the crime. At one time, there was authority that evidence of a man's homosexuality was admissible on a charge of indecent assault to rebut the defence of innocent association[19] or to prove identity.[20] That view was rejected in *Boardman* and followed by the Supreme Court of Canada in *R. v. Morin.*[21] There it was held by Mr. Justice Sopinka that there must also be some further distinguishing feature:

> Accordingly, if the crime was committed by someone with homosexual tendencies, it is not sufficient to establish that the accused is a practising homosexual, or indeed is engaged in numerous homosexual acts. The tendered evidence must tend to show that there was some striking similarity between the manner in which the perpetrator committed the criminal act and such evidence.[22]

---

17 (1982), 1 C.C.C. (3d) 149, 31 C.R. (3d) 261 (Ont. C.A.).
18 *R. v. McNamara (No.1)* (1981), 56 C.C.C. (2d) 193 (Ont. C.A.).
19 *R. v. King (Dennis Arthur)* (1966), 51 Cr. App. R. 46 (C.A.).
20 *R. v. Glynn* (1971), 5 C.C.C. (2d) 364, 15 C.R.N.S. 343 (Ont. C.A.).
21 (1988), 41 C.C.C. (3d) 193, 66 C.R. (3d) 1 (S.C.C.).
22 *Ibid.*, at 23 (66 C.R. (3d)).

6

Opinion Evidence

1. THE RULE

A witness is not allowed to express his personal belief or give his opinion about a fact in issue unless the matter calls for his special skill or knowledge and he is an expert in such matters. This rule is based on the notion that it is possible to draw a distinction between a fact and the inference to be drawn from that fact. Witnesses are supposed to testify as to matters which they observe through their senses, that is, eyes, ears, nose, etc. It is for the jury to decide what is the proper inference to be drawn from the facts established by a witness.

The difficulty with the rule is that it is not always easy to draw a line between fact and opinion. For example, when a witness says that "the car was going very fast" or that "the accused was angry" or that "the girl was very pretty" or that "the person is very old," the witness is really expressing his personal opinion based on his own experience and view of matters. Yet such evidence is given frequently in court without objection. Indeed, in an Ontario case, *R. v. German*,[1] a witness was allowed to give evidence that the accused was intoxicated. Chief Justice Robertson justified the reception of that evidence in this way:

> No doubt, the general rule is that it is only persons who are qualified by some special skill, training or experience who can be asked their opinion upon a matter in issue. The rule is not, however, an absolute one. There are a number of matters in respect of which a person of ordinary intelligence

---

1 [1947] O.R. 395, 89 C.C.C. 90, 3 C.R. 516 (C.A.).

may be permitted to give evidence of his opinion upon a matter of which he has personal knowledge. Such matters as the identity of individuals, the apparent age of a person, the speed of a vehicle, are among the matters upon which witnesses have been allowed to express an opinion, notwithstanding that they have no special, qualifications, other than the fact that they have personal knowledge of the subject matter, to enable them to form an opinion.[2]

Not all courts, however, have adopted this liberal approach to the general rule. For example, in *R. v. Browne and Angus*,[3] the question was whether a witness could identify a person as the perpetrator of a crime. O'Halloran J.A. argued:

> A positive statement "that is the man", when rationalized, is found to be an opinion and not a statement of single fact. All a witness can say is, that because of this or that he remembers about a person, he is of opinion that person is "the man". A witness recognizes a person because of a certain personality that person has acquired in the eyes of the witness. That personality is reflected by characteristics of the person, which, when associated with something in the mind of the witness, causes the latter to remember that person in a way the witness does not remember any other person.

> Unless the witness is able to testify with confidence what characteristics and what "something" has stirred and clarified his memory or recognition, then an identification confined to "that is the man", standing by itself, cannot be more than a vague general description and is untrustworthy in any sphere of life where certitude is essential.[4]

Nevertheless, the courts have continued to allow an ordinary witness to give evidence on a "subject about which most people should be able to express an opinion from their ordinary day-to-day experience of life." These include such matters as disputed handwriting if the witness has acquired previous knowledge of the handwriting of the person whose handwriting is in dispute,[5] the age of another person, his own mental or physical condition, whether a person is intoxicated or impaired by alcohol, the degree of intoxication and whether the person's ability to drive is impaired,[6] and estimates of such things as speed, distance, size, etc.

2. EXPERT OPINION

An exception to the rule exists in favour of witnesses who are classified as experts. The theory underlying expert testimony is that experts, because

---

2 *Ibid.*, at 409-410.

3 (1951), 99 C.C.C. 141, 11 C.R. 297 (B.C. C.A.).

4 *Ibid.*, at 147.

5 *R. v. Derrick* (1910), 5 Cr. App. R. 162 (C.C.A.).

6 *R. v. Graat* (1982), 2 C.C.C. (3d) 365, 31 C.R. (3d) 289 (*sub nom. R. v. Gratt*) (S.C.C.).

of their knowledge, training and experience, are able to form better opinions on a given state of facts than opinions formed by those not so well equipped (such as ordinary jurors). Their opinions are admitted in evidence to aid the jury in understanding questions which inexperienced persons are not likely to decide correctly without such assistance. If the subject is one of common knowledge and the facts can be intelligibly described to the jury, and they can form a reasonable opinion for themselves, the opinion of an expert will be rejected.

An expert is therefore someone who is qualified, by study or experience, to form a definite opinion of his own respecting a division of science, branch of art or department of trade, which persons having no particular training or special study are incapable of accurately forming. It is not a university degree which makes a person an expert; it is his special knowledge by study or practical experience.

On the other hand, the fact that a witness may have knowledge about a subject and may understand it better than the judge or jury does not necessarily justify receiving his evidence. If the judge or jury can become sufficiently informed about the subject during the trial so that they can reach an accurate conclusion, there is really no basis for the expert opinion.

Once the witness is qualified by the court to give expert testimony, then he may be permitted to express his opinion on the conclusion which should be drawn from certain facts. He may have personal knowledge of the facts but, more often than not, he will have none whatsoever. In this instance, he will be asked to give his opinion on what is called a hypothesis or a hypothetical question. He will be asked to assume certain facts which will be outlined to him. He will then be asked for his opinion on the conclusion that should be drawn from those facts respecting matters which are within his special training in that field. It should be stressed that the expert is only entitled to give his opinion on the facts. If the answer involves a conclusion of law, he is not entitled to give his opinion.

The opinion of the expert is premised upon the truth of the facts which he knows or assumes hypothetically. Those assumed facts must be established by evidence in the regular way, otherwise the basis of the expert's opinion collapses. Indeed, the judge must warn the jury and instruct himself that before the opinion can be considered, they must be satisfied as to the truth of the facts upon which the expert is relying. An attack on the facts assumed by the expert is usually one of the ways a cross-examiner will attempt to discredit the expert's opinion.

One of the most common complaints concerning expert evidence is that the witness is giving his opinion on the very issue which the judge and jury must decide. For example, if the issue is whether the accused was insane, a psychiatrist called as an expert will be asked whether the accused was capable of "appreciating the nature and quality of his acts" or "of knowing that his acts were wrong" in accordance with section 12 of the Criminal Code.

Although it has often been said that opinion evidence is not admissible on the very question that the jury has to decide otherwise it will usurp their function, this statement fails to recognize the reality of expert testimony. It is only natural for the jurors, thrust into the unfamiliar environment of the courtroom, to rely heavily on what an expert has to say.

It is sometimes said that where the facts are disputed, an expert may not express an opinion on the ultimate issue because the opinion depends on the witness's assessment of the evidence.[7] This view, however, fails to recognize that when an expert is asked to give his opinion based on assumed hypothetical facts, the validity of that opinion depends upon the correctness of the facts. For example, if a psychiatrist is of the opinion that the accused is insane within the meaning of section 12 of the Criminal Code and has based that opinion on certain assumed facts, there is no reason why he cannot give his opinion as to the accused's insanity although it is an opinion on the ultimate issue, that is, that the accused is insane. If it turns out that those facts are not correct, then his opinion collapses. In such instance, the main responsibility lies with the judge to properly instruct the jury that before they can consider the weight of the expert's opinion, they must first be satisfied of the factual assumptions underlying that opinion.

Nevertheless, the courts have always had difficulty with the application of the ultimate issue rule. For example, in *R. v. Lupien*,[8] the accused was charged with gross indecency. His defence was that he thought that the male person with whom he was found was, in fact, a female, and attempted to introduce psychiatric evidence to show that he had a strong aversion to homosexual practices and therefore would not knowingly engage in homosexual acts. The Supreme Court of Canada was divided on the issue.

The dissenting judges felt that the psychiatric opinion ought not to be admitted because it came too close to the very question that the jury had to decide on the whole of the evidence. The majority view, however, was that the expert testimony was admissible on the question of whether or not the man was "homosexually inclined or otherwise sexually perverted." Mr. Justice Hall gave these reasons:

> That type of evidence is very close, if not identical, to the conclusion the jury must come to in such a case if it is to find that the accused was not guilty because he did not have intent necessary to support conviction. The weight to be given the opinion of the expert is entirely for the jury, and it

---

7 *R. v. Swietlinski* (1978), 44 C.C.C. (2d) 267 at 301, 5 C.R. (3d) 324 (Ont. C.A.).
8 [1970] S.C.R. 263, [1970] 2 C.C.C. 193, 9 C.R.N.S. 165.

is the function of the trial judge to instruct the jury that the responsibility for weighing the evidence is theirs and theirs alone.[9]

The real difficulty facing the jury occurs when two experts express diametrically opposed views. This means that their decision will turn not on which facts are proved in evidence, but on which expert the jury believes. The result is that the decision will then depend more on which expert is credible than on whose opinion is the correct one. One solution to the problem may be for the court to intervene and appoint its own expert.

---

9 *Ibid.*, at 280.

7

Admissions and Confessions

1. THE RULE

A confession is defined as a statement either in writing or given orally by a person accused of a crime which shows or tends to show that he is guilty of the crime with which he is charged. An admission is said to be distinguishable from a confession because it is only an acknowledgment of a material fact that may form a link in the chain of proof against the accused. Unlike a confession, an admission need not necessarily be in writing or made orally; it can also include conduct that could reasonably be taken to be intended as an assertion.[1] The simplest example of an admission by conduct occurs when a police officer asks the accused if the murder weapon belongs to him and he nods his head affirmatively. No words have been spoken but his conduct is sufficient to constitute an admission that the weapon belongs to him.

Some legal scholars regard admissions and confessions as exceptions to the hearsay rule; others say that they are not because they are not offered to prove a fact in issue, but only to impeach the credibility of the accused. The first view is probably correct. Admissions and confessions are

---

1 *R. v. St. Lawrence* (1949), 93 C.C.C. 376, 7 C.R. 464 (Ont. H.C.).

exceptions to the hearsay rule because it is only logical to assume that what a person says against his own interest is probably true.

The distinction between a confession and an admission is not important when it comes to the rule relating to their admissibility. Both are governed by the same rule which was stated by Lord Sumner in *Ibrahim v. R.*[2] and judicially endorsed in Canada by the Supreme Court of Canada in *Boudreau v. R.*:

> It has long been established as a positive rule of English criminal law, that no statement by an accused is admissible in evidence against him unless it is shown by the prosecution to have been a voluntary statement, in the sense that it has not been obtained from him either by fear of prejudice or hope of advantage exercised or held out by a person in authority. The principle is as old as Lord Hale.[3]

There are three reasons for this rule. The first is the concern that a confession following an inducement may be false. The second reason is a more emotional one. Until the middle of the seventeenth century, it was common practice for the ecclesiastic courts to compel anyone suspected of committing a crime against the security of the state to attend before a government official and to take an oath, called the *"ex officio* oath,"* to tell the truth to all questions that might be put to him. He was not told of the specific crime nor the names of the witnesses. If he told the truth, he might find himself charged with a crime which would put his life in peril. If he lied, he was charged with perjury and imprisoned. If he said nothing, he was arrested, tortured and incarcerated. It was not until the famous *Lilburne* case in 1641 that the *ex officio* oath was abolished and it was recognized that no man should be required to incriminate himself — *"nemo tenetur prodere se ipsum"* or *"nemo tenetur prodere accusare."*

There is a third reason why the courts will reject a confession that has been obtained under circumstances which indicate that it is not voluntary. It is important that the public have confidence in the way that police carry out their duty to investigate crime. Unless the court is satisfied that the confession of an accused is free and voluntary, there is the concern that the public will believe that oppressive tactics are regularly used by the police. This will result in a loss of support and respect by the community for the criminal justice system.

2. FORMAL ADMISSIONS

At common law, an accused was not permitted to make a formal admission where he was charged with a felony; nor is it certain that he

---

2 [1914] A.C. 599 (P.C.).

3 [1949] S.C.R. 262 at 281, 94 C.C.C. 1, 7 C.R. 427.

could even do so where the charge was a misdemeanour. Section 655 of the Criminal Code has altered that rule. It permits an accused charged with an indictable offence to "admit *any fact* alleged against him for the purpose of dispensing with proof thereof" (emphasis added).

Does section 655 permit the defence to admit the voluntariness of a confession? The voluntariness of a confession is a question of law and is, strictly speaking, not something that can be admitted because section 655 only permits admissions of fact. However, trial judges have been able to get around this dilemma by having the accused admit that all of the facts leading up to the taking of the statement are consistent with it being voluntary.

Although the admission is characterized as a factual one, it does have legal consequences. However, in *Park v. R.*,[4] the Supreme Court of Canada went so far as to suggest that the defence has the right to waive the usual *voir dire* held to consider the voluntariness of the statement, and the trial judge has the wide discretion to accept that waiver if he is satisfied that the statement is voluntary.

3. ADMISSIONS BY CONDUCT

If we can assume that what a person says against his own interest is probably true and should be admitted against him, it follows that how he responds when an incriminating statement is made in his presence should be admissible against him if his actions or conduct are indicative of guilt.

Let us assume, for example, that Constable Jones, who is investigating a charge of assault, confronts the accused, Brown, and tells him that he has reasonable grounds to believe that he has just assaulted Smith. If Brown responds by punching the officer and running away, it would be natural to assume that his conduct is indicative of guilt and should be admissible against him. However, if Brown responds by denying the charge, as one would expect an innocent person to do, then his denial is not admissible at the instance of the defence because it is self-serving. This contradiction is often difficult to accept.

Silence of the accused creates another problem. Although silence in the face of an accusation might cause one to ask why an innocent person has not denied his guilt, the law does not permit that response to be admitted because an accused's right to silence is a constitutional guarantee. It would be unfair if the exercise of that right became a way to trap someone into an admission of guilt.[5]

---

4 (1981), 59 C.C.C. (2d) 385, 21 C.R. (3d) 182 (S.C.C.).

5 *R. v. Eden*, [1970] 3 C.C.C. 280 (Ont. C.A.).

The problem arises because in *R. v. Christie*,[6] it was held by the House of Lords that that in some circumstances even a denial of an accusation might amount to an acknowledgment of its truth. One might question how a denial of an accusation could ever amount to an adoption of it unless the denial turns out to be an untrue statement. If this occurs, the prosecution might be able to use the denial to attack the accused's credibility to show that it is inconsistent with a prior or subsequent statement made by him.

The real difficulty arises where the accused's response is ambiguous and open to interpretation. Should the trial judge refuse to admit the response, or should he admit it and leave it to the jury to draw their own conclusions? Unfortunately, the courts have offered little guidance. For example, in *R. v. Fargnoli*,[7] the accused was arrested for indecently assaulting his daughter and when asked whether he wished to say anything replied, "You got it all there . . . there is nothing more for me to say about it." Two members of the Ontario Court of Appeal held that the response amounted to an acceptance of the facts while the third dissented, holding that the response was ambiguous and out not to have been admitted.

4. THE MEANING OF VOLUNTARY

If one applies the *Ibrahim* rule strictly, it means that no statement can be admitted if it was obtained as a result of a threat or a promise. The law does not require that the threat be openly made. Words or conduct which would lead an accused to believe that violence will be used against him if he does not confess will amount to a threat. Even a veiled promise of punishment will amount to a threat. This is why it is important for the judge to look at all of the surrounding circumstances before he considers the effect of the words or conduct of the police officer.

Words such as "it would be better for you if you told us what happened" or "you will be arrested if you do not tell us where the stolen goods are" or "you had better tell us the truth" or "it is necessary to give an explanation" have all been held to constitute a threat. Words such as "be sure to tell the truth" and "be a good girl and tell the truth" have been held not to constitute a threat. The reason is that the first group of words are an expression of compulsion or obligation to speak whereas the second are not. However, the dividing line is often difficult to draw and this is why it is important to look at the context in which the words are used.

The background of the accused himself is also a relevant factor. Someone who has never been involved with the police before may be so terrified by the predicament in which he finds himself that he may be

---

6 [1914] A.C. 545 (H.L.).

7 (1957), 117 C.C.C. 359, 23 C.R. 310 (Ont. C.A.).

more influenced by suggestions made by a police officer than an experienced criminal would be.

A promise or inducement is anything that gives the accused some hope or expectation with respect to the charge or contemplated charge or to some other matter. That "some other matter" could be another charge against the accused or a charge against someone whom the accused might wish to help, such as his wife or child or a close friend. A promise or inducement could result, not only from the police officer's words, but also from a combination of his words and those of the accused. If an accused asked the police officer whether he would be released "if I give a statement," the officer's affirmative reply could constitute an inducement. Any suggestion by a police officer that he will offer the accused assistance could constitute an inducement if it evokes a confession from the accused.

For forty years after *Ibrahim*, the courts applied the rule so strictly that exclusion occurred only where there was an actual threat or inducement. However, in 1956, the Supreme Court of Canada in *R. v. Fitton*[8] finally recognized the role which compulsion or oppression could play in causing someone to make a statement. Mr. Justice Rand expressed it this way:

> The rule on the admission of confessions . . . at times presents difficulty of application because its terms tend to conceal underlying considerations material to a determination. The cases of torture, actual or threatened, or of unabashed promises are clear; perplexity arises when more subtle elements must be evaluated. The strength of mind and will of the accused, the influence of custody or its surroundings, the effect of questions or of conversation, all call for delicacy in appreciation of the part they have played behind the admission, and to enable a Court to decide whether what was said was freely and voluntarily said, that is, was free from the influence of hope or fear aroused by them.[9]

This passage recognizes that oppressive conditions may cause a person to feel compelled to make a confession. Oppressive conditions have a tendency to sap a person's free will, which is a necessary element of a voluntary confession. Since each individual has a unique psychological make-up, a court must examine all of the conditions surrounding the taking of the statement, such as the length of the period of questioning, the length of time intervening between periods of questioning, whether the accused was given proper refreshment, and the individual characteristics of the accused. As has been noted:

> What may be oppressive as regards a child, an invalid or an old man or somebody inexperienced in the ways of this world may turn out not to be

---

8 (1956), 116 C.C.C. 1, 24 C.R. 371 (S.C.C.).

9 *Ibid.*, at 5.

oppressive when one finds that the accused person is a tough character and an experienced man of the world.[10]

In 1979, the Supreme Court of Canada took the *Ibrahim* rule even further. In *Ward v. R.*, Mr. Justice Spence wrote:

> In my view, there is a further investigation of whether the statements were freely and voluntarily made even if no hope of advantage or fear of prejudice could be found in consideration of the mental condition of the accused at the time he made the statements to determine whether or not the statements represented the operating mind of the accused.[11]

Ward, who had been involved in a single car collision, was found lying unconscious outside his vehicle. His lady friend was found dead beside him. After being revived by mouth to mouth resuscitation at the scene of the accident, Ward was questioned by police officers but denied driving the vehicle. Thirty minutes later and again some five or six hours later at the hospital, he was questioned and this time admitted driving the vehicle. He was charged with criminal negligence.

On the *voir dire*, Ward said that he could not remember anything from the time that he was in a hotel some hours before the accident until the afternoon or evening following the accident. His doctor testified that he could answer simple questions but was unable to tell them what had happened. The Court held that the trial judge was correct in excluding Ward's responses because they did not represent his "operating mind."

A similar result was reached in *Horvath v. R.*[12] Horvath, a youth of 17, was charged with the murder of his mother. On the evening of his arrest, he was interrogated and cross-examined by two police officers for two and one-half hours, but the statement he gave contained nothing inculpatory. The next day, he was interviewed by another officer, who was a skilled interrogator, for four hours except for three brief intervals. Horvath, who was left alone during those three intervals, was observed by the officer reflecting aloud in what were called "monologues" or "soliloquies." During the second monologue, he admitted killing his mother and repeated the confession to the officer. In the third monologue, he asked his mother's forgiveness for having disclosed the incident. He then signed a confession.

The trial judge, however, rejected the confession after accepting the opinion of a psychiatrist that Horvath had been in a hypnotic state for a large part of the interview before he signed the confession. In a split decision of the Supreme Court of Canada, it was held that the confession, which had followed directly from the earlier statement, and which was

---

10 Note to Martin Priestly (1967), 51 Cr. App. R. 1.
11 (1979), 44 C.C.C. (2d) 498 at 506, 7 C.R. (3d) 153 (S.C.C.).
12 (1979), 44 C.C.C. (2d) 385, 7 C.R. (3d) 97 (S.C.C.).

made while under hypnosis, was not voluntary because it had been induced by conditions created earlier.

Recently, a new consideration has entered into the voluntary test: whether the accused was aware of what was at stake in making any statement. In *R. v. Clarkson*,[13] the accused, while intoxicated, had confessed to the police to murdering her husband. The trial judge excluded the statement because he was not satisfied that the accused was "aware of the consequences" of making the statement. His decision was upheld by the Supreme Court of Canada, but only two of the seven judges agreed with the trial judge's reasons. Although the remaining judges held that the accused had been deprived of her right to counsel, they did not reject the "awareness of the consequences" test. It was held that it was up to the trial judge, in his unique position of hearing all of the witnesses, to consider the issue when balancing the probative value of the evidence in light of the possible prejudice to the accused.

5. PERSONS IN AUTHORITY

It may be remembered that the *Ibrahim* rule said that a confession of an accused is not admissible unless it is voluntary in the sense that it was not obtained by a threat or promise held out by "a person in authority." If the person is not someone in authority, then the rule does not apply and the confession will be admissible.

There are no authorities which clearly define who is or who is not a "person of authority." A number of cases, however, have held that certain people such as police officers, gaolers or guards, magistrates or judges, prosecutors, informants or complainants, employers and building inspectors, are persons in authority. It may be said, as a general rule, that a person in authority will include anyone who has authority or control over the accused or over the proceedings or prosecution against him.[14]

On the other hand, persons such as physicians, surgeons and psychiatrists, the father or wife of the accused, or a friend, have been held not to be persons in authority. However, if someone such as a doctor or a psychiatrist is called in by the Crown to examine the accused, that person will be considered a person in authority because he has a role in the prosecution of the accused.

For along time, a perplexing question was whether a subjective or an objective test should be used in determining if the person was someone "in authority." In other words, was it enough that the person was someone in authority or was it necessary for the accused to believe as well that

---

13 (1986), 25 C.C.C. (3d) 207, 50 C.R. (3d) 289 (S.C.C.).
14 *R. v. Todd* (1901), 13 Man. L.R. 364, 4 C.C.C. 514 (C.A.).

he was a person in authority? One would have thought that the answer was self-evident, at least in the case of inducement. How can a person be affected by an inducement unless he believes that the person has the ability to make good his promise? The case of a threat or a beating is another matter. Here a confession would be rejected by a trial judge in exercise of his discretionary power to prevent the administration of justice from being brought into disrepute rather than from the rules relating to persons in authority.

Nevertheless, that question was never settled until the decision of the Supreme Court of Canada in *R. v. Rothman.*[15] There the Court held that the test was a subjective one. The real issue was whether the accused thought that the person to whom he confessed could either make good his promise or carry out his threats. Thus, if the accused confessed to someone such as an undercover officer, then that officer was not a person in authority even though he might be, from a purely objective point of view, considered to be in a position of undoubted authority.

6. THE ONUS OF PROOF

Where the prosecution seeks to introduce a confession or admission, the trial judge will generally conduct a *voir dire*, that is, a trial within a trial, and exclude the jury while he considers the voluntariness of the statement. On the *voir dire*, the prosecution is entitled to call evidence to establish the voluntariness of the statement. The defence is entitled to cross-examine the prosecution witnesses and to call witnesses on behalf of the defence including the accused who may, in turn, be cross-examined by the prosecution. After hearing argument from both sides, the judge will decide whether the statement should be admitted.

If the accused elects to testify on the *voir dire*, he may be cross-examined on the particular issue in dispute, that is, whether the statement is voluntary. This has been held to include the right to ask him whether the confession is true because it goes to the issue of his credibility.[16] This decision of the Supreme Court of Canada has been strongly criticized because it does "under the guise of 'credibility' . . . transmute what is initially an inquiry as to 'admissibility' of the confession into an inquisition of an accused."[17]

Moreover, the argument that the prosecution should be allowed to test an accused's credibility by asking him on a *voir dire* whether the confession is true, is a double-edged sword. If he denies the truth of the

---

15 (1981), 59 C.C.C. (2d) 30, 20 C.R. (3d) 97 (S.C.C.).

16 *DeClercq v. R.*, [1969] 1 C.C.C. 197, 4 C.R.N.S. 205 (S.C.C.).

17 *R. v. Hnedish* (1958), 29 C.R. 347 at 349-350 (Sask. Q.B.).

statement, is he to be disbelieved simply because he contradicts the testimony of the police? On the other hand, if he admits that the confession is true, is he to be disbelieved when he says that it was obtained by threats or violence? One could argue more persuasively that if he admits that the confession is true, this tends to show that he tells the truth and should be believed when he says that the police used violence or inducements to obtain it from him. Moreover, if he does admit that the confession was true, this places the trial judge in the difficult position of having to exclude an important piece of evidence obtained under circumstances which the administration of justice does not condone, even though he knows that it is true.

The onus of proof lies upon the Crown to satisfy the court beyond a reasonable doubt that the statement is voluntary in the sense described earlier. It is not enough for the prosecution to simply call the interrogating officers, establish that the confession was preceded by the usual caution or warning, and then have the officers who took the statement say that it was made freely and voluntarily.[18] The general rule is that the prosecution must call all persons who had anything to do with the accused during the period before the statement was made and during his interrogation, or at least make them available for cross-examination.[19]

There is no requirement that a confession be admitted only after a *voir dire*, where the Crown has established the voluntariness of the statement beyond a reasonable doubt. In *Park*,[20] the Supreme Court of Canada recognized that an accused or his counsel could waive or dispense with the holding of *voir dire* where the voluntariness of a confession was not in dispute. The decision whether or not to hold a *voir dire* lies with the trial judge. He may, if he is satisfied that no objection is taken to the admission of the statement without a *voir dire*, or that voluntariness is not in issue, admit the statement without a *voir dire*.

7. THE RIGHT TO COUNSEL

Section 10 of the Canadian Charter of Rights and Freedoms guarantees:

10. Everyone has the right on arrest or detention
(a) to be informed promptly of the reasons therefore;
(b) to retain and instruct counsel without delay and be informed of that right.

Whenever an accused is detained or arrested, he must be informed

---

18 *R. v. Sankey* (1927), 48 C.C.C. 97 (S.C.C.).
19 *Thiffault v. R.* (1933), 60 C.C.C. 97 (S.C.C.).
20 *Supra*, note 4.

of his right to retain and instruct counsel. Except in the case of a young offender, the mentally or physically infirm, and possibly someone who has had no experience with the police, that duty is simply to advise the accused of his right to counsel and to provide him with the opportunity to contact his lawyer if he so requests. It is not necessary to satisfy the court that the detained or arrested person understood his rights, unless there are circumstances that would lead him to believe otherwise. It is generally presumed that a person understands the meaning of the right to counsel unless that person can establish otherwise.[21]

Once a person who has been advised of his right to counsel indicates that he wishes to exercise that right, the police officer questioning him must stop until that request is fulfilled.[22] If he ignores that request, any statement obtained will be excluded at trial under section 24(2) of the Charter.

However, an accused who requests the right to counsel cannot delay indefinitely consulting with him. He must take reasonable steps to try to contact his lawyer to obtain advice. If he fails to do so, then the police may proceed to question him.[23]

A person may waive his right to counsel and that waiver need not be in writing. However, the onus of establishing that the accused waived his right to counsel, with full knowledge of the consequences of doing so, lies upon the prosecution. That may be particularly onerous if it appears that the accused does not have his full faculties, such as an accused who may be mentally ill or under the influence of drugs or alcohol.[24] In the *Clarkson* case, the Supreme Court of Canada held:

> While this constitutional guarantee cannot be forced upon an unwilling accused, any voluntary waiver in order to be valid and effective must be premised on a true appreciation of the consequences of giving up the right.[25]

The police are not required to stop all questioning after an accused has consulted with his lawyer. They may question him provided that he is willing to be questioned. They are not required to advise his lawyer that they are about to question him because, presumably, the lawyer has advised his client of this right. The issue is really one of waiver. If an accused consents to be questioned after consulting a lawyer, then there is nothing objectionable in doing so. However, the prosecution must establish, as in any case where the right to counsel has been waived, that the accused agreed to the interrogation without the presence of his lawyer.

---

21 *R. v. Anderson* (1984), 10 C.C.C. (3d) 417, 39 C.R. (3d) 193 (Ont. C.A.).
22 *R. v. Manninen* (1987), 34 C.C.C. (3d) 385, 58 C.R. (3d) 97 (S.C.C.).
23 *R. v. Tremblay* (1987), 37 C.C.C. (3d) 565, 60 C.R. (3d) 59 (S.C.C.).
24 *Clarkson, supra,* note 13.
25 *Ibid.,* at 219.

PART III

Proof at Trial

8

Proof

1. GENERALLY

The common law system is known as the adversarial or accusatorial system, as opposed to the continental system which is described as the inquisitorial system. Although both systems have many characteristics in common, such as an oral hearing with both the prosecution and the accused separately represented by counsel, and with no compulsion upon the accused to answer questions, there are distinct differences. Under the inquisitorial system, the judge takes an active role in questioning witnesses for the prosecution and examining the accused and witnesses for the defence. Moreover, prior to trial, a brief or dossier compiled by a juge d'instruction or examining magistrate containing the examination of various witnesses is provided to the judge and jury.

The common law system may be more described as a duel between the Crown prosecutor and the defence counsel, with the judge sitting in the middle as an impartial arbiter. There are, however, some limitations placed upon the contestants. It is the duty of counsel for the Crown to bring all of the facts both for and against the accused before the court. Moreover, it has been said that:

> ... the business of counsel for the Crown is fairly and impartially to exhibit all the facts to the jury. The Crown has no interest in procuring a conviction.

>Its only interest is that the right person should be convicted, that the truth
>should be known, and that justice should be done.[1]

On the other hand, it is the duty of counsel for the defence to use all of the legitimate means at hand to obtain an acquittal for his client.

The steps in the process are as follows: opening statement by the prosecution; presentation of the prosecution's case; opening statement by the defence; presentation of the evidence for the defence; rebuttal evidence by the prosecution; summation of counsel for the prosecution and for the defence; charge to the jury by the trial judge; verdict.

2. THE CASE FOR THE CROWN

In a jury trial, but not necessarily in a trial by judge alone, the prosecution will begin with an opening speech to the jury. The purpose of the speech is to lay before the jury a brief summary of the facts upon which the prosecution relies to establish its case and of the evidence that it expects each prosecution witness will give. The Crown must always be fair in the opening address, as well as in the prosecution in general. There is a duty to be impartial and to guard against injecting comments likely to excite or inflame the jury against the accused.

When the address is completed, the trial judge will call upon the prosecution to present its case. Witnesses will then be called by the Crown to be examined in chief. In an examination-in-chief, the prosecution must be careful not to lead the witness on matters crucial to its case. A leading question is one which suggests the answer to the witness. For example, it is not permissible to ask the witness, "Did you see the accused shoot the victim?" A leading question may also be one which takes for granted evidence that a witness has not yet given. The question, "When did you stop beating you wife?" is leading because it assumes that the witness has already said that he beat his wife in the past and has stopped doing so.

When the prosecution has completed its examination-in-chief, the defence may cross-examine the witness. The purpose of cross-examination is to show that the witness is mistaken or lying, or it may be directed towards bringing out facts favourable to the defence. Here, questions which suggest the answer are not only permitted, but will often be put to the witness by the cross-examiner.

When the defence has completed the cross-examination of the witness, then Crown counsel will be permitted to re-examine the witness. The purpose of re-examination is to clarify matters which were raised by the

---

1 *R. v. Sugarman* (1935), 25 Cr. App. R. 109 at 114-115 (C.C.A.), *per* Lord Hewart C.J.

defence during cross-examination. In re-examination, counsel for the prosecution is not entitled to bring out new facts unless they were raised by the defence during cross-examination, and only to reply to those new facts. The Crown is not entitled to rehash or simply go over again evidence already given.

If a witness gave evidence at the accused's preliminary hearing or at a previous trial on the same charge but now refuses to give evidence or to be sworn, or is dead, insane, too ill to travel or to testify, or is absent from Canada, section 715 of the Criminal Code permits the witness's evidence to be read as evidence in the trial. However, the trial judge may refuse to permit the evidence to be read if he is satisfied that the accused did not have full opportunity to cross-examine the witness.

If the Crown has presented a *prima facie* case, that is, evidence upon which a jury properly instructed could convict the accused, then the trial judge will call upon the defence to present its case. If the prosecution has failed to establish a *prima facie* case, then counsel for the defence is entitled to move for a directed verdict of acquittal. If the judge agrees that a *prima facie* case has not been established, he will direct the jury that, as a matter of law, they must acquit the accused. He will explain to them that it is not a factual issue for them to decide but a legal issue, and they must accept his direction because he is the final arbiter on the law. The jury may retire to consider the verdict or may consult without retiring and render its verdict. The latter is the usual practice. In trials by judge alone, the judge will simply dismiss the charge.

3. THE REQUIREMENT FOR CORROBORATION

Although it is often said that the common law system is distinguishable from the civil law system because the court is entitled to reach a decision on the unsupported evidence of one witness, that is not the way it always was. In its infancy, the jury system required that a certain number of persons swear upon oath that an accused was guilty or not guilty, although it might be said that the witnesses were really giving evidence as to the accused's character rather than probative evidence on the question of his guilt or innocence. Later, as the jury system became more like what we know it today, certain rules developed. One was the requirement that no prosecution for treason could succeed upon the evidence of one witness; another was that a prosecution for perjury required clear corroborating testimony. A rule of practice also developed requiring the corroboration of the testimony of complainants in sexual cases, accomplices and children.

Support for the corroboration of women was based on the belief that:

> . . . these cases are particularly subject to the danger of deliberately false

charges, resulting from sexual neurosis, phantasy, jealousy, spite or simply a girl's refusal to admit that she consented to an act of which she is now ashamed.[2]

For the corroboration of children, it was argued that:

Children are suggestible and sometimes given to living in a world of make-believe. They are egocentric, and only slowly learn the duty of speaking the truth . . . a child's power of observation and memory tends to be even less reliable than that of an adult.[3]

In the last decade, the requirement for corroboration of the testimony of women, children and accomplices has been swept away either by legislation or case law.[4] The only surviving requirement for corroboration arises in prosecutions for treason (section 47(3) of the Criminal Code), perjury (section 133), forgery (section 367(2)), and procuring a feigned marriage (section 292(2)). This does not mean that, apart from these offences, a judge is never required to warn the jury about evidence which may be suspect.

In *R. v. Vetrovec*, Chief Justice Dickson suggested that what might be appropriate:

. . . in some circumstances, is a clear and sharp warning to attract the attention of the juror to the risks of adopting, without more, the evidence of the witness.[5]

The need for some helpful direction, as he pointed out, was particularly important in lengthy trials where guilt or innocence would depend upon the acceptance or rejection of the evidence of one or more witnesses, or in cases involving accomplice evidence or disreputable witnesses.

As has been noted, there can be no conviction for treason, perjury, forgery or procuring a feigned marriage on the evidence of one witness unless that evidence is "corroborated in a material particular by evidence that implicates the accused." Corroborative evidence is thus independent, confirmatory evidence of the witness which shows or tends to show not only that a crime was committed, but also that the accused committed it. The law is that the trial judge is required to specify for the jury what items of evidence are capable of being corroborative, leaving to them the ultimate question of deciding whether such items are, in fact, corroborative. If items viewed cumulatively, (but not alone), are capable of constituting corroboration, the trial judge must specify those items which may be considered part of the cumulative package.[6]

---

2 Glanville Williams, *The Proof of Guilt*, 3rd ed. (London: Stevens & Sons, 1963) at 159.
3 *Ibid.*, at 178-179.
4 *R. v. Vetrovec* (1982), 67 C.C.C. (2d) 1, 27 C.R. (3d) 304 (S.C.C.).
5 *Ibid.*, at 17.
6 *R. v. McNamara (No. 1)* (1981), 56 C.C.C. (2d) 193 (Ont. C.A.).

4. THE CASE FOR THE DEFENCE

If there is some evidence upon which a jury, properly instructed, can convict the accused, the judge will call upon the defence to present its case. The defence may or may not call evidence. If the defence elects to call evidence, it is entitled to make an opening address to the jury. The purpose of the opening address is to put before the jury essentially what the defence is all about and what the defence witnesses, including the accused if it is intended to call him, are expected to say.

If witnesses are called by the defence, the proceedings are reversed. The witnesses will be examined in chief by counsel for the defence, or the accused if he is unrepresented, cross-examined by counsel for the Crown, and re-examined by counsel for the accused.

5. REBUTTAL EVIDENCE FOR THE PROSECUTION

The general rule as to the order of proof is that the prosecution must introduce all evidence in its possession that it relies upon to establish its case before it closes its case. The rule is intended to prevent an accused from being taken by surprise and to enable him to investigate by cross-examination the reliability of such evidence before he is called upon to introduce his defence. It is also intended to prevent the undue emphasis or magnification of evidence in relation to other evidence by reason of its late introduction.[7]

Thus, rebuttal evidence is restricted to only that evidence needed to meet new facts presented by the defence. But, the accused's mere denial of the prosecution's case during the course of his testimony does not constitute new facts permitting the prosecution to repeat its case or to introduce additional evidence to support it. However, the trial judge does have the discretion to admit, in reply, evidence relevant to the Crown's case as a result of defence evidence which the prosecution could not reasonably be expected to anticipate.

An example where rebuttal evidence was introduced was the case of *R. v. Sparrow*,[8] a murder case. There, the accused's car was found containing shell cartridges from the same type of gun used to kill the deceased. Blood stains from the same grouping as the deceased were also found on the car's trunk. During the course of his cross-examination, the accused "guessed" that the blood stains were the result of a fist fight between the deceased and a friend several days before the killing. The Crown was allowed to call in reply a professor of "criminalistics" to testify

---

7 *R. v. Campbell* (1977), 38 C.C.C. (2d) 6, 1 C.R. (3d) 309 (Ont. C.A.).

8 (1979), 51 C.C.C. (2d) 443, 12 C.R. (3d) 158 (Ont. C.A.).

as to the age of the blood stains because the issue was not a live one until the accused testified.

6. ADDRESSES OF COUNSEL AND JURY CHARGE

When all of the evidence is completed, counsel are entitled to address the jury or, in the case of trial by judge alone, the judge. The rule is that if the defence has called any evidence, including the accused, the defence is required to address the jury or judge first. If the defence has called no evidence, then the usual practice is for the Crown, at the conclusion of its case, to address the jury or judge. This will then be followed by counsel for the defence.

In his charge to the jury, the judge is required to review the evidence with them and instruct them on the law which they are to apply to that evidence. He will, of course, stress that while they are the sole judges of the facts and the weight to be given to the evidence presented, he is the final judge of the law and they must take their law from him. Upon the completion of his charge, the jury will then retire to consider their verdict.

In the case of a judge alone, the judge may deliver his verdict at the conclusion of argument by counsel or he may reserve and deliver his judgment at a future time.

9

Presumptions and Burdens of Proof

1. PRESUMPTIONS GENERALLY

Everyone involved in the field of criminal law knows that there is a presumption that a person accused of a crime is innocent and that there is a burden of proof upon the Crown to establish the guilt of an accused beyond a reasonable doubt. These well-known examples of presumptions and burdens of proof, however, do not easily explain the distinction between the two.

We might take instruction from the definition offered by Chief Justice Dickson of the Supreme Court of Canada in *R. v. Oakes*:

> In determining the meaning of these words, it is helpful to consider in a general sense the nature of presumptions. Presumptions can be classified into two general categories: presumptions *without* basic facts and presumptions *with* basic facts. A presumption without a basic fact is simply a conclusion which is to be drawn until the contrary is proved. A presumption with a basic fact entails a conclusion to be drawn upon proof of the basic fact.

> Basic fact presumptions can be further categorized into permissive and mandatory presumptions. A permissive presumption leaves it optional as to whether the inference of the presumed fact is drawn following proof of the basic fact. A mandatory presumption requires that the inference be made.

> Presumptions may also be either rebuttable or irrebuttable. If a presumption

is rebuttable, there are three potential ways the presumed fact can be rebutted. First, the accused may be required merely to raise a reasonable doubt as to its existence. Secondly, the accused may have an evidentiary burden to adduce sufficient evidence to bring into question the truth of the presumed fact. Thirdly, the accused may have a legal or persuasive burden to prove on a balance of probabilities the non-existence of the presumed fact.

Finally, presumptions are often referred to as either presumptions of law or presumptions of fact. The latter entail 'frequently recurring examples of circumstantial evidence' . . . while the former involved actual legal rules.[1]

Presumptions are really aids to assist a court in determining the issue before it. They are not, in themselves, either evidence or argument, although they may be based on general experience or probability, or even on policy and convenience. A few examples using the categories outlined by Chief Justice Dickson may be of assistance.

Section 354(1) of the Criminal Code makes it an offence for anyone to have in his possession any property knowing that it was obtained by the commission in Canada of an indictable offence. To succeed on this charge, the Crown must establish the following: (1) the accused had the property in his possession; (2) the property was obtained by the commission in Canada of an offence punishable by indictment (usually stolen); and (3) the accused knew that it was obtained by the commission in Canada of an indictable offence, in other words, that he knew that it was stolen.

The doctrine of recent possession, a common law rule, states that where an accused is found in possession of goods proved to have been *recently* stolen, the judge or jury, as the case may be, may infer not only that he had possession of goods knowing them to have been stolen, but also that he participated in whatever offence was committed by which the goods were obtained. In the prosecution of the accused, all that the Crown must establish is that the goods were found in the possession of the accused and that they were recently stolen. Common experience tells us that people in possession of goods that were recently stolen or obtained illegally should have some knowledge about how they were obtained.

The law then casts upon these people a presumption of guilty knowledge unless, during the course of the trial, an explanation is offered. The rule is that the judge must tell the jury (or himself if he is trying the case alone) that they *may*, not that they must, in the absence of an explanation that might reasonably be true find the accused guilty.[2] Even if no explanation is offered whatsoever, the judge or jury are entitled to find the accused guilty but are not required to do so.

This is a permissive presumption. It leaves optional the question of

---

1   (1986), 24 C.C.C. (3d) 321 at 330-331, 50 C.R. (3d) 1 (S.C.C.).

2   *R. v. Ungaro* (1950), 96 C.C.C. 245 (S.C.C.).

whether the inference of the presumed fact (that is, guilty knowledge) should be drawn following proof of the basic fact (possession by the accused of goods recently stolen). It does not require the inference to be drawn.

Another example may be of assistance in understanding what is meant by a mandatory presumption. Section 354(2) of the Criminal Code specifically provides that where an accused is found in possession of a motor vehicle that has the identification number wholly or partially obliterated, two presumptions will arise. The first is that the vehicle was obtained by the commission of an indictable offence; the second is that the accused knew that the vehicle was obtained by the commission of an indictable offence. However, this statutory presumption, unlike the common law doctrine of recent possession, is a mandatory presumption of law because section 354(2) provides that where the basic facts are established, (possession of a motor vehicle by the accused with the identification number wholly or partially obliterated), this will amount to "proof" that the accused had the vehicle in his possession *knowing* that it was obtained by the commission of an indictable offence. Unlike a permissive presumption, a mandatory presumption requires the judge or jury to conclude that the presumed fact has been established unless there is evidence to the contrary. It is true that the evidence to the contrary need only raise a reasonable doubt. However, if the accused fails to raise a reasonable doubt, the judge is required to instruct the jury that they *must*, not simply may, convict the accused.[3]

Before leaving this area two important presumptions should be discussed briefly.

2. SPECIFIC PRESUMPTIONS

(a) The Presumption of Innocence

The presumption of innocence has been long recognized under the common law. In *Woolmington v. Public Prosecutions Director*, Viscount Sankey L.C. wrote:

> Throughout the web of the English Criminal Law one golden thread is always to be seen, that it is the duty of the prosecution to prove the prisoner's guilt subject to what I have already said as to the defence of insanity and subject also to any statutory exception. If, at the end of and on whole of the case, there is a reasonable doubt, created by the evidence given by either the prosecution or the prisoner . . . , the prosecution has not made out the case and the prisoner is entitled to an acquittal. No matter what the charge or where the trial, the principle that the prosecution must prove the guilt of

---

3 *R. v. Boyle* (1983), 5 C.C.C. (3d) 193, 35 C.R. (3d) 34 (Ont. C.A.).

the prisoner is part of the common law of England and no attempt to whittle it down can be entertained.[4]

That principle has received international recognition in the Universal Declaration of Human Rights adopted December 10, 1948 by the General Assembly of the United Nations and by the International Covenant on Civil and Political Rights, 1966, article 14(2). It has also been given constitutional guarantee in Canada by section 11(d) of the Canadian Charter of Rights and Freedoms. That section provides:

11. Any person charged with an offence has the right

(d) to be presumed innocent until proven guilty according to law in a fair and public hearing by an independent and impartial tribunal.

The right simply means that there is no obligation upon an accused to respond either by giving evidence personally or by calling other witnesses. The burden is on the Crown to prove the accused's guilt beyond a reasonable doubt.

(b) The Presumption of Sanity

Section 16(1) of the Criminal Code provides that "no person shall be convicted of an offence in respect of an act or omission on his part while that person was insane." However, section 16(4) goes on to provide that "everyone shall, until the contrary is proved, be presumed to be and to have been sane." Both the Crown and the defence have the right to raise the question of the accused's insanity. Whoever raises it, however, must bear the burden of proof. That burden is to establish the insanity of the accused on a balance of probabilities, as opposed to beyond a reasonable doubt. It has been held that this shift of onus to the accused to prove insanity is not an unconstitutional infringement of the presumption of innocence as guaranteed by section 11(d) of the Charter.[5]

3. BURDENS OF PROOF

The close relationship between presumptions and burdens of proof often make it difficult to distinguish between the two. It is probably easier to state what the burden of proof is rather than to define it. In a dispute between parties, the burden of proof is the evidentiary burden which the court imposes on one side or the other. The general rule is that the burden

---

4 [1935] A.C. 462 at 481-482 (H.L.).

5 *R. v. Godfrey* (1984), 11 C.C.C. (3d) 233, 39 C.R. (3d) 97 (Man. C.A.), leave to appeal to S.C.C. refused (1984), 11 C.C.C. (3d) 233n (S.C.C.).

of proof lies on the party who asserts the affirmative of the issue or question in dispute. The extent of that burden will vary depending on the nature of the trial.

For example, in a civil trial, where A is suing B for breach of contract, the burden of proof is on A to establish that breach. In civil cases, the onus is simply on a balance of probabilities. The most vivid example of that onus is the tipping of scales slightly in favour of the person who has the burden. If A tips the scales in his favour, ever so slightly, he wins. If the scales are tipped in favour of B or are evenly balance, then A loses because he has failed to discharge the burden.

In a criminal case, the burden is always on the prosecution and never shifts to the accused. The burden is also more onerous. That burden is to establish the guilt of the accused beyond a reasonable doubt.

4. CONSTITUTIONAL GUARANTEES

As was pointed out earlier, section 11(d) of the Charter guarantees any person charged with an offence the right "to be presumed innocent until proven guilty according to law in a fair and public hearing by an independent and impartial tribunal." Since the enactment of that section, there have been a number of cases in Canada attacking presumptions, both permissive and legal, as breaching section 11(d). These presumptions, described as reverse onus provisions, have been attacked on the basis that they have whittled down the presumption of innocence. The position of the Crown in these cases has generally been that these presumptions have been created by statute because there is a close connection between the basic fact and the presumed fact. Unless the presumption is allowed to stand, there may be instances where the Crown will be unable to prove its case. Thus, it is argued that section 1 of the Charter protects presumptions as a reasonable limit in a free and democratic society.

In *R. v. Oakes*,[6] the Supreme Court of Canada set out the test which should be applied in determining whether or not a section of a statute which breached the Charter was saved by section 1. One of those considerations was whether the measures adopted were carefully designed to achieve the objective in question. In other words, a presumed fact in a statute could not be saved by section 1 unless it was rationally connected to the basic fact. In the *Oakes* case, the defence argued that section 8 of the Narcotic Control Act,[7] which requires an accused found in possession of a narcotic to disprove on a balance of probabilities that he had the narcotic in his possession for the purpose of trafficking, violated section

---

6 *Supra*, note 1.
7 R.S.C. 1985, c. N-1.

11(d) of the Charter and was not saved by section 1. The Court agreed with the argument. It was held that there was no rational connection between the basic fact of possession and the presumed fact of possession for the purpose of trafficking since the reverse onus clause could give rise to unjustified and erroneous convictions for drug trafficking of persons guilty only of possession of a small quantity of narcotics. Section 8 was held to be unconstitutional as infringing the presumption of innocence in section 11(d).

In *R. v. Boyle,* discussed earlier, the Court of Appeal of Ontario considered the rationality of the connection between the basic fact (possession of a motor vehicle with a wholly or partially obliterated identification number) with the two presumed facts (that the vehicle was obtained by the commission of an indictable offence and that the accused had guilty knowledge) and found the first presumed fact constitutionally valid but not the second. It was held that the only conceivable reason for removing or obliterating a vehicle identification number was to conceal the fact that it had been stolen or had been obtained by the commission of an indictable offence. On the other hand, since the presumption of guilty knowledge was not restricted to persons such as car dealers, who might reasonably be presumed to be knowledgeable with respect to the location of vehicle identification numbers and to be alive to the desirability of making an examination to ascertain whether there had been obliteration of such numbers, there was no rational connection between the basic fact and the presumed fact.

Index